guide to KNOTS

guide to KNOTS

knots • bindings • loops • bends • shortenings • hitches

Geoffrey Budworth

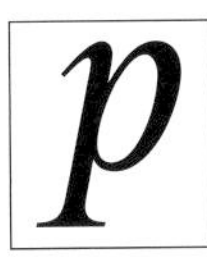

This is a Parragon Publishing book

First published in 2005

Parragon Publishing
Queen Street House
4 Queen Street
Bath BA1 1HE, UK

ISBN: 1-40545-028-2

A copy of the CIP data for this book is available from the British Library upon request.

The rights of Geoffrey Budworth to be identified as the author of this work have been asserted in accordance with Section 77 of the Copyright, Designs and Patents Act of 1988.

Created, designed, produced, and packaged by
Stonecastle Graphics Ltd

Designed by Paul Turner and Sue Pressley
Edited by Philip de Ste. Croix
Knot diagrams by Malcolm Porter
Knot photography by Roddy Paine

Printed and bound in China

The author and publishers have made every reasonable effort to contact all copyright holders. Any errors that may have occurred are inadvertent and anyone who for any reason has not been contacted is invited to write to the publishers so that a full acknowledgement may be made in subsequent editions of this work.

Photographs on pages 10, 46–47, 50, 56, 64, 72–73 © Stonecastle Graphics Ltd
Photograph on pages 98–99 © Mike Dobson

WARNING

This book is a simple introduction to knot tying. Do not use any of the knots, bends, and hitches featured for activities involving predictable risk of loss, damage, or injury, until you have first sought the advice and guidance of qualified practitioners and obtained from them appropriate training and equipment.

Never loop ropes, or tie knots, around the neck of anyone and always ensure that lengths of rope and cord are safely coiled and stored out of the reach of children.

It is all too easy while tying or tightening a fishing knot to impale finger or thumb upon the barbed point of a fishing hook. To avoid this nasty accident, mask the point with a bit of rubber eraser, cork, Blu-Tack®, or some sort of modelling material, such as Plasticine®, before starting to tie knots to them.

Contents

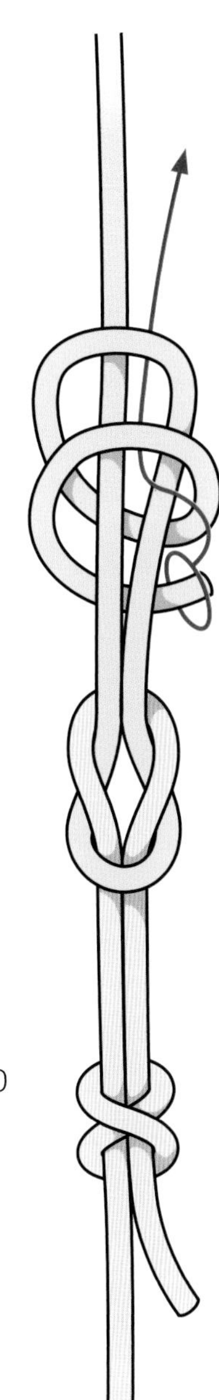

Introduction

There is no other field of human activity where we happily teach techniques that are thousands of years old ... Every other human endeavor has changed drastically over the centuries, but we still rely on many of the same techniques in knotting as those used by our distant ancestors.

(Richard Hopkins, *Knots*, 2003)

Everyone should know how to tie a knot or two ... or ten. If you cannot yet do so, that is merely because you have not learned how. And now is the best time to remedy this omission, as knotting has become a lively field of endeavor, keenly pursued by an increasing number of devotees of both sexes and all ages.

Nobody should be totally reliant upon factory-made clips, clamps, clasps, and other gadgets, when a knotted lace or lashing will do at least as well – often better. For this reason knot tyers, a resourceful and self-sufficient lot, are rarely without cord in their pockets.

Learn only a handful of the knots described in this book, use them often, and you will become a different person. As a knotting *aficionado* you will never be at a loss when faced with needing to apply a life-saving first aid tourniquet, attaching a tow-line to a broken-down vehicle, or flying a kite on a string. Astronauts and zoologists (and every trade or calling alphabetically in-between) ought to know the ropes and how to knot them.

Anyway, all practicalities aside, knotting is an enjoyable recreation, as absorbing as doing a jigsaw puzzle or solving a crossword. Knotting is also a creative pastime, and skilled knotters can use their expertise to produce stunning artwork, decoration, and jewelry from cord and string.

Because a disproportionate number of the brain's neural connections are involved with tasks requiring manual dexterity, knotting can also be therapeutic. The recovery of several stroke victims, for example, is said to have been helped by the practice of tying knots.

Knotting can be an art, a craft, and a science (all beyond the scope of this introductory book) about which we may still know less than half of what remains to be discovered. Knot theory is a sub-field of topology (multi-dimensional geometry) and, in 1990, the New Zealand professor Vaughan Jones, FRS, was awarded a Fields Medal – the mathematicians' equivalent of a Nobel Prize – for his fruitful research in this abstruse and esoteric area, where the Jones polynomial has become a useful tool.

A brief history of knots

From the Stone Age to the Space Age, knots have enabled humankind to survive, flourish, and develop. Today knotting is enjoying a quantum leap as new tools, techniques, and theories are devised or discovered. Of the more than 500 books on knotting that are recorded, at least 20 percent have been published in the last 20 years. However, the earliest to feature knots were 18th- and 19th-century seamanship manuals.

Right: *South American vaqueros and Western American cowboys often learned how to tie some knots one-handed while on horseback.*

Below: *Knots and splices – their application and subsequent maintenance – occupied sailors during both routine voyages and awesome sea battles.*

In the beginning knots predated fire, farming, the wheel, wind-power, and maybe even human speech. Cave dwellers and hunter gatherers no doubt tied knots.

Peering back into the Paleolithic, we find fragmentary evidence of early folk contriving knots, using fibrous roots, rawhide thongs, and twisted cords of gut, grass, or hair with which to

haul and hoist loads, stitch and lash together clothes and shelter, snare game and net fish for food, immobilize injured limbs, seize and bind enemies, and strangle human sacrifices.

The builders of prehistoric megalithic monuments, medieval stone strongholds and magnificent temples of worship, all had need of knotted ropes. Later, so too did the civil engineers on such projects as Tower Bridge in London, England, and the Hoover (or Boulder) Dam across the Colorado River between Arizona and Nevada in the USA.

Ropes also enabled restless and curious humankind to scale mountains, cross chasms, and descend into caves and gorges. On the field of battle, the outcome of some confrontations and conquests was decided in part by the bowstring knots of archers.

Nautical knots, often fancy but always functional, evolved to secure the hempen rigging of square-rigged sailing ships during what is – with romantic hindsight – perceived to have been a glorious Age of Sail (and cordage). What is less well known is that South American *vaqueros* and western American cowboys subsequently tied even more complicated knots in their rawhide and leather horse harnesses as well as plaited horsehair watch-chains and love tokens.

Cordage terms and materials

The catch-all term for every kind of spun and twisted or braided material is **cordage**, although it may be referred to casually as **stuff** (for instance, 'cheap stuff,' 'strong stuff,' or 'unusual stuff'). Anything over about 0.4in (10mm) diameter is **rope** while a rope for a specific use becomes a **line** (washing line, fishing line, throwing line). Thinner stuff is **cord**, while thinner still is **twine** or **thread** or **string**.

Note
The moderately priced cordage sold in DIY and hardware stores is good for many domestic and trade purposes – including learning to tie knots – but bear in mind, that it will not have the same high-performance specifications as the much more expensive specialized ropes sold in camping and climbing stores or by yacht chandlers.

Synthetic cordage

Most kinds of cordage today are synthetic – products that are not naturally occurring but created by chemists. Those most commonly marketed and sold are the four 'P's, namely:

- **Polyamide** (generally known as nylon)
- **Polyester** (otherwise terylene and dacron)
- **Polyethylene** (polythene)
- **Polypropylene**

All are strong, durable, and resistant to attack by mildew, rot, and vermin. Nylon, however, loses up to 15 percent of its strength when wet but recovers when dry again. Polyester is a little weaker than nylon, but it remains the same wet or dry. Polypropylene – unless specially treated – does not withstand UV radiation well and will degrade if over-exposed to the Sun's rays.

Nylon stretches, absorbing the extra energy of severe and sudden loading, and so reduces the risk of exceeding its breaking strength. This makes it suitable for tow-ropes, some climbing ropes, mooring ropes, and fishing lines, all of

***Below:** Shrouds, halyards, stays, and other such ropes are part of the scene at any crowded harbor.*

which must withstand shock-loading of one kind or another. When the load is removed, nylon regains its original length.

Polyester, by contrast, has little elasticity and this may be deliberately removed by pre-stretching during the manufacturing process. Use it for applications where stretch is undesirable, such as the shrouds, stays, and standing rigging that support masts and similar vertical structures, as well as for the halyards, mainsheets, and other running rigging rove through blocks or assembled as tackles and purchases.

Polypropylene is weaker than either nylon or polyester, but it is cheaper and it floats. Being buoyant, it is made into ski tow-lines, throwing lines, and the lifelines securing those emergency lifebelts found beside water in public places.

Above: *Life-support knots must always be strong and secure, easily learned, and readily tied.*

Below: *Fishing knots are one of the few items of tackle which anglers must make themselves.*

Other 'super fibers' are weight-for-weight stronger than wire or steel ropes and the stuff of spiders' webs. These include:

- **Kevlar, Twaron, and Technora** which are aramid derivatives
- **Spectra or Dyneema** HMPE or high modulus polyethylene (UV stable)
- **Vectran** LCP or liquid crystal polymer thermoplastic
- **Zylon** PBO or poly(p-phenylene-3,6 benzo-bisoxazole)

The remarkable performances of these comparative newcomers to the cordage scene are matched by equally breathtaking prices per foot. They have some weaknesses – such as poor resistance to abrasion, low flex fatigue, and vulnerability to UV radiation – but the manufacturers combat such problems by sheathing these exotic products in a braided polyester outer covering.

CAUTION

Every sort of synthetic rope and cord will melt and part if subjected to heat that exceeds known melting points, which are approximately:

Nylon = 482°F (250°C)
Terylene or Dacron = 473°F (245°C)
Polypropylene = 302°F (150°C)
Polyethylene = 262°F (128°C)
Dyneema or Spectra = 329°F (165°C)
Vectran = 932°F (500°C)

However, beware – they will all glaze, fuse, and weaken at lower temperatures, so keep such cordage away from campfires (even flying sparks) and avoid heat-generated friction.

Below: *Laid, braided, or sheath-and-core – and matt or shiny – the extraordinary variety of synthetic cordage is as diverse as hi-tech research and development and modern manufacturing processes can achieve.*

__Above:__ White, brown, or darker still – soft and flexible or hard and hairy – natural fiber cordage is vintage stuff evoking a mostly bygone age.

Natural fiber cordage

This is made from organic material of vegetable or animal origin, as all cordage was until around 60 years ago. In many parts of the world it is still widely used, although less so by the industrialized nations. However, such products add variety to knotting so do not scorn them. The raw materials for this sort of rope-making are obtained from:

- the fibrous stems of plants (such as flax, hemp, and jute)
- leaves (for example, manila and sisal)
- the fibers attached to seeds and husks (cotton, coir)

Other vegetable fiber sources include date palms, tree bark, reeds, and esparto grass. Materials of animal origin include gut, hair, silk, and wool.

All natural fiber cordage must be carefully dried before being hung up in ventilated storage as – unlike synthetic stuff – it is vulnerable to mildew, rot, and predation by vermin.

Hemp is one of the strongest and most durable of natural fiber ropes, but **manila** has greater resistance to rot when wet. **Sisal** is a cheap substitute for both. **Coir** is stretchy and withstands immersion in salt water, which is why (although it has only a quarter of the strength of manila) it is made into 'grass rope' throwing lines and is fitted to some traditional hire boats and other small craft in the form of fenders.

Cordage construction

Depending upon the tension imparted by the rope-making machines, cordage may be **soft-laid** (floppy, flexible, and really good for learning, practicing and demonstrating knots) or **hard-laid** (tight, stiff, and less easy to tie in knots).

The traditional image of a rope (*see diagram right*), whether natural fiber or synthetic, is of three **strands** which spiral in a clockwise direction and are said to be **Z-laid** or **right-handed**. Look closely at the individual strands of a Z-laid rope and you will see how each one consists of a bundle of **yarns** which are S-laid (the opposite of the rope itself); and these yarns are themselves made from Z-laid **fibers** (the opposite of the strands). This alternating twist and counter-twist creates the rope's characteristic cohesion, geometry, and performance. The somewhat dated nautical term for the construction of such a rope is **hawser-laid**.

Rope laid up counter-clockwise is **S-laid** or **left-handed** or **shroud-laid** (another almost obsolete nautical term).

Three Z-laid hawsers may be laid up to together to form an S-laid **cable** of nine strands.

Not much natural fiber rope is braided. Synthetic cordage, by contrast, more often than not consists of an inner core encased in an outer braided sheath. Unlike the naturally occurring short and irregular fibers of animal or vegetable origin, the basic elements of synthetic cordage are either:

- **monofilaments** larger than 0.002in (50 microns) in diameter, or
- **multifilaments** less than 0.002in (50 microns) in diameter.

Both of these components are continuous and uniformly round in cross-section. Consequently synthetics are inherently smooth and shiny, unlike rough natural cordage which has all its fiber ends projecting from the surface. This can make knot tying in modern cordage problematic due to lack of grip. Many synthetics, however, are roughed-up and given a matt finish with a desirable fuzzy feel during the production process. Another way to reproduce the hairiness

of natural fiber cordage is to chop the extruded and practically endless synthetic filaments into short lengths, imitating staple plant fibers, and cordage made this way is marketed as **staplespun**.

Another comparatively cheap and cheerful synthetic rope is made from polypropylene film, shredded, combed, and twisted into what are known as **split-film** ropes.

The outer covering of braided cordage can consist of eight, 16, or 32 bundles of parallel monofilaments or multifilaments plaited together. The core itself may be laid up into three strands; or it can be braided; or it can be simply a bundle of parallel yarns. Such ropes (*see F, G, H and J below*) are collectively called **sheath-and-core** or **braid-on-braid**. Cordage that lacks a core is appropriately known as **hollow braid**.

To achieve greater flexibility, eight strands can be plaited together, the resulting cable going by the trade-name 'Octoplait.' Cables can also be plaited with 12 strands.

Above: *Examples of a variety of synthetic cordage showing the construction of each type*

A) *3-strand, 6mm, pre-stretched red polyester*

B) *3-strand, 10mm diameter, navy nylon*

C) *3-strand, 12mm, white polyester hawser*

D) *3-strand, 12mm, blue polypropylene*

E) *3-strand, 14mm, brunette polyester 'hempline'*

F) *5mm, black (with pink flecks) polyester sheath and Dyneema core*

G) *8mm, red, matt polyester sheath-and-core*

H) *12mm, white with blue and gold flecks, matt polyester braid-on-braid*

I) *12mm, navy blue nylon 'octoplait'*

J) *16mm, white (with blue flecks), polyester braid-on-braid*

Care of cordage

> **CAUTION**
> Hot melted cordage is sticky. Take care it does not adhere to skin and burn it. Also, as the fumes from some synthetics are unpleasant and could be harmful if inhaled, work in a well-ventilated place.

Avoid foreseeable risk to life and property by ensuring that ropes are well-preserved, not damaged or defective, worn or weak. And remember, cordage is never cheap and can be very costly, so it makes sense to look after it.

Here are some basic rules which will help to ensure that your cordage is always in tip-top condition:

- Protect cordage from rough treatment of any kind
- Minimize unavoidable abrasion and friction
- Keep cordage away from oil and grease, dirt, grit, and strong chemicals
- Avoid extremes of cold and heat
- Limit exposure to direct sunlight
- Wash and rinse cordage periodically
- Dry natural fiber ropes thoroughly
- Inspect all load-bearing ropes for obvious signs of weakness – cut and frayed fibers; a wrinkled or ruptured outer sheath; glazing or fusing due to heat friction
- Prise open hawser-laid and cable-laid ropes to look for deterioration or damage of internal strands, yarns, and fibers;
- Assess the likely condition of sheath-and-core or braid-on-braid ropes, whose flawless outer coverings may conceal dangerous internal damage. Those with a history of hard work, or just one severe stress, should be downgraded to less crucial work (like learning, practicing, and teaching knots)

Coiling

Small diameter cords can be folded and wrapped in handily stored hanks, but rope should be kept in coils. Z-laid ropes must be coiled clockwise (*see diagrams opposite*) and a small clockwise twist imparted as each 360-degree circle is added. This cures the coil of its innate tendency to writhe and tangle. For the same reason S-laid ropes must be coiled counter-clockwise, with counter-clockwise twists. Sheath-and-core or braid-on-braid cordage can generally be coiled either way.

The accumulated twist inserted during coiling will – when a coiled rope is run out once more – reappear, but in a correctly coiled rope this will not be too severe. In Z-laid (or S-laid) ropes coiled the wrong way, however, severe kinking almost inevitably occurs.

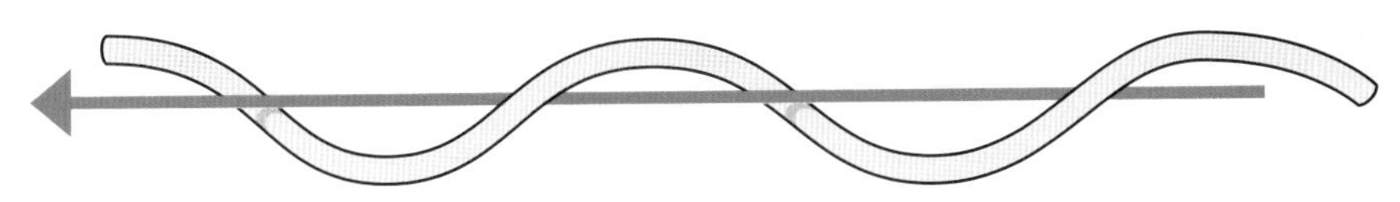

In Z-laid lines a clockwise coil runs out more freely...

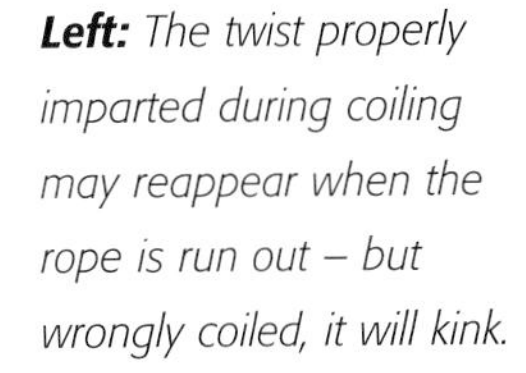

Left: *The twist properly imparted during coiling may reappear when the rope is run out – but wrongly coiled, it will kink.*

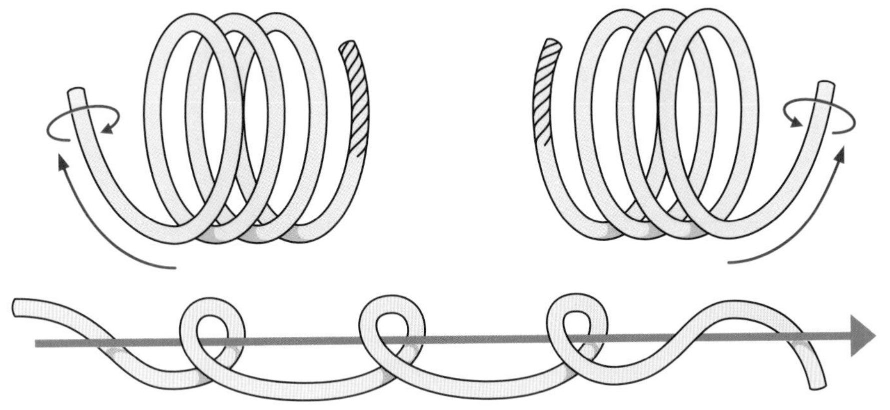

...than a counter-clockwise coil, which may kink.

Below: *Three alternative first-aid treatments for the cut ends of ropes – (from left to right) whipped, taped, and heat-sealed.*

Heat-sealing, taping, tying, or whipping

Ropes fray and unravel when cut. Synthetics, lacking the cohesion of natural fiber cordage, are worse in this respect. Do not allow this to happen. Tie a constrictor or double constrictor knot (*see pages 22–25*) either side of the place where a rope is to be severed, before doing so. Alternatively, wrap adhesive tape either side of where the cut will be located. Otherwise, whip cut ends (*see page 26*).

Synthetic cordage can be cut and sealed at the same time – doing away with the need for taping, tying, or whipping – by the application of heat. Simply apply the flame from a lighted match or cigarette lighter to string, twine, or thin cords, and burn through them. Thicker cords and ropes should be sliced through with a heated knife blade. Cordage retailers, professional rope workers, and keen amateurs use a purpose-made electric guillotine, which can be either bench-mounted or hand-held.

Knot names and terms

Alpine butterfly, figure-eight loop, Munter mule – are they Olympic figure-skating maneuvers, or the latest diabolical computer viruses? In fact, they are knot names. Knotting is a craft which has its own helpful – but highly specialized – jargon.

There are thousands of different knots and uncountable variations of some kinds of them. All, however, can be allocated into one of three main groups, namely:

- **Bends** which join the separate ends of ropes or cords in such a way that they can be untied later
- **Hitches** attaching one end of a line to a rail, ring, spar, or post (or another rope)
- **Knots** which include anything that is not a bend or hitch

The all-embracing label 'knot' brings together fixed **loops**, adjustable or slide-and-grip **nooses**, **bindings**, **shortenings**, and **stopper knots**.

You do not need to know the name of any individual knot in order to learn and use it, but it helps to know their names when talking with other knot tyers, and becomes essential when reading and writing about them. Knotty nomenclature can, however, help or hinder.

A knot's name may suggest its

- appearance (figure-eight stopper knot, round turn and two half-hitches)
- use (hoisting hitch, knife lanyard knot)
- user (angler's loop, surgeon's knot)

A name may imply – rightly or wrongly –

- the region of origin (Alpine butterfly loop, Italian hitch)
- originator (Ashley's stopper knot, Tarbuck knot).

Some knots have evocative names (perfection loop, Zeppelin bend), while several have over time acquired more than one designation (the figure-eight stopper knot is also described in print as the Flemish knot).

NOTE

The standing part of any rope used to be called 'the bight,' which is why knots in the middle of a rope – made without using either end – are still said to be 'tied in the bight.' Today, however, the term **bight** tends to be limited to a doubled, U-shaped tongue or rope or cord. Although bights at the end of a line may have knots tied in them – for example, the overhand loop (*see Life-Support Knots*) – this is NOT, strictly speaking, tying in the bight … it is merely tying *with* a bight or the doubled end of a line. Knots tied *in* the bight, strictly speaking, do not need ends. Confusing? Well, part of the fun in learning knots is picking up such arcane fragments of knot lore.

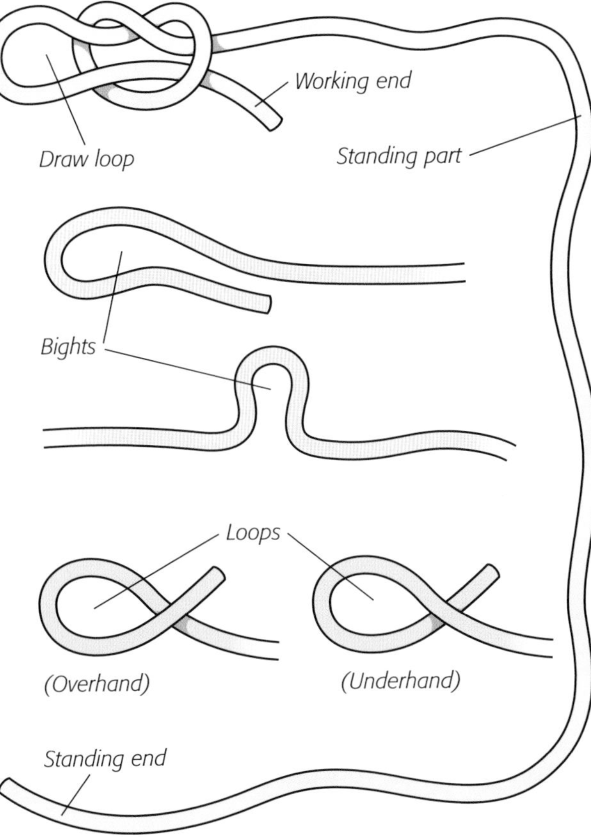

Tying terms (*see diagram above*)
Pick up a length of rope or cord to make any knot and the end with which you tie that knot is termed the **working end**. The other inert end is the **standing end**. Everything between these two extremes is the **standing part**.

Impart a half-twist to a bight and the result is a **loop**. Loops may be **overhand** (when the working end is placed on top) or **underhand** (when it lies underneath).

A knot impatiently or carelessly tightened will be a weak and unreliable knot. Tightening is as important as the tying process and should be performed with as much thought and care. Only a few knots (for instance the double reef bows in shoe laces) can be tightened by simply tugging. Most knots must first be **dressed**, that is, molded into their final form with one's finger tips. Only then can tightening begin with careful removal of slack and daylight from the knot by pulling, a bit at a time, upon each end or strand that emerges from the knot to bed it down. Finally, when each turn and tuck is snug and neat, give each end and strand a parting tug to conclude the tightening process.

Buying cordage
The only stuff you need with which to learn and practice the knots featured in this book is a couple of six foot (two-meter) lengths of braided cord between no more than 0.4 inch (5-10mm) in diameter. They should be soft-laid, and they could be different colors.

If you buy anything else for some practical purpose, then bear in mind that (comparing like with like) a thicker rope is stronger than a thinner one, twice as thick being four times as strong. Braids are stronger than strands, and synthetic cordage is stronger and more durable than natural fiber – so it can be thinner. Do not buy cordage that is bigger and better quality – and consequently more expensive – than you need for the job in hand.

MULTI-PURPOSE KNOTS

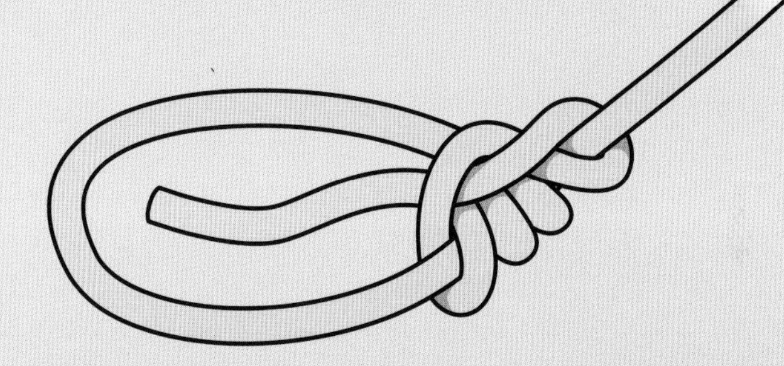

Most knots are multi-purpose and separating them into different sections results in some arbitrary decisions. Do not be misled. Many – if not all – of those grouped together as Boating Knots and Life-Support Knots would be just as effective doing other things. Only fishing knots are, perhaps, so specialized that they do not easily adapt from nylon monofilament lines to thicker, coarser cordage. Even that is not always true, however, because the offshore swivel knot (for example) is well-known to dock and construction workers as the hook sling called a cat's paw; and the perfection (or angler's) loop is so versatile that it has been included in this section as a multi-purpose knot, rather than being grouped with Fishing Knots where, historically, it belongs.

Constrictor knot

Expert tip
To remove a constrictor that does not have a draw-loop, simply sever the overlying diagonal knot part with a sharp blade, and the cord will fall away in two curly segments.

The constrictor is a tenacious binding knot, applied to the cut ends of ropes as a first-aid alternative to whipping. It will hold a hose on a tap or keep joinery joints together while the glue dries, and can even be used to tether a pencil or ballpoint pen to a clipboard.

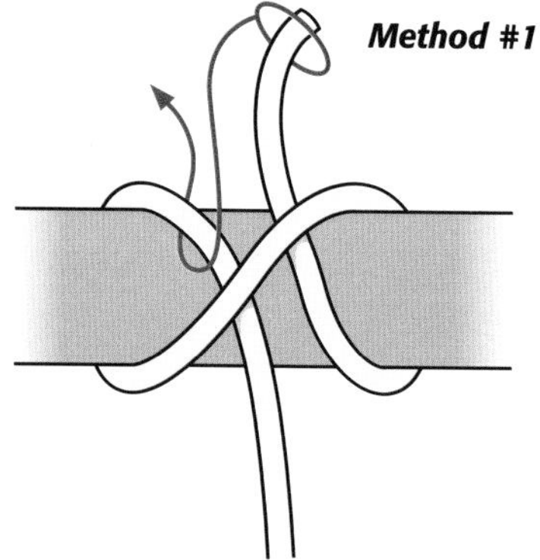

Method #1 (tying with an end)

1 *To tie a constrictor to a ring or long rail, first take a turn with the working end and lead it diagonally over itself, in this instance from SW to NE. Then take a second turn and tuck the end beneath the diagonal to create a letter 'N' shape.*

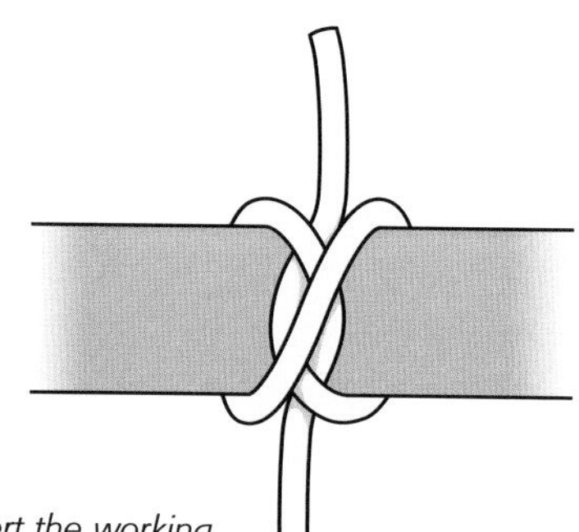

2 *Finally divert the working end to tie a simple half-knot with the inert end. Tighten the knot by pulling on both ends, so that the overriding diagonal pins and holds the half knot, after which the ends may be cut off close to the knot for extra neatness.*

Knot lore
There is documentary evidence that a knot resembling the constrictor – and perhaps identical to it – was used in Ancient Greece as a surgical sling.

Method #2 (tying in the bight)

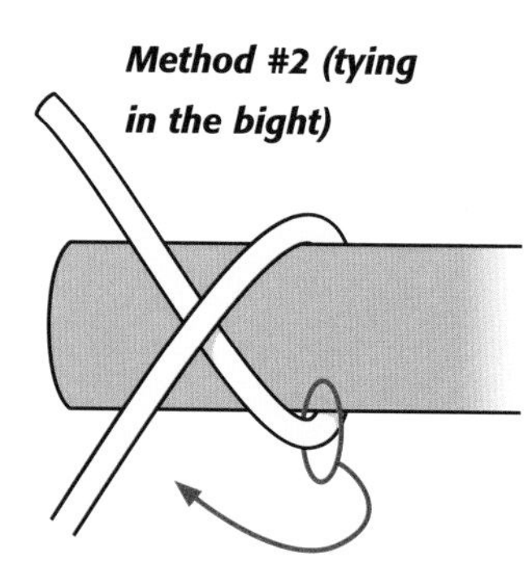

1 *Where possible, tie a constrictor 'in the bight' (that is, without using an end). First slip a turn onto the rope's end or whatever else is to be seized.*

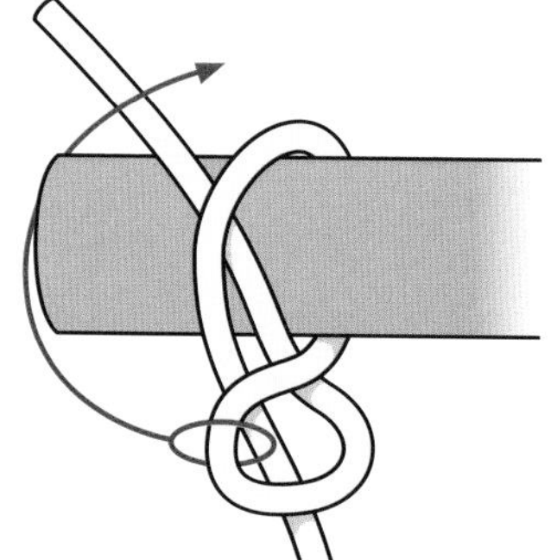

2 *Next, locate and pull out a bight from the lower part of that turn.*

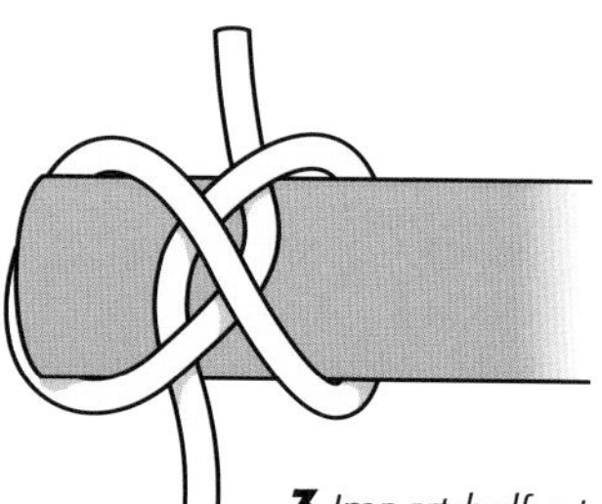

3 *Impart half-a-twist to the loop and place it over the end of the foundation. Tighten the knot and trim off both ends.*

Double constrictor knot

When the foundation to be tied has a large diameter – for instance, if a bight is to be seized to form a loop – the constrictor's grip may be overstretched. In which case, a double constrictor (or two) may be preferable to its troubled sibling.

Expert tip
To cut off a double constrictor, sever both overlying diagonal knot parts with a sharp blade.

Method #1 (tying with an end)

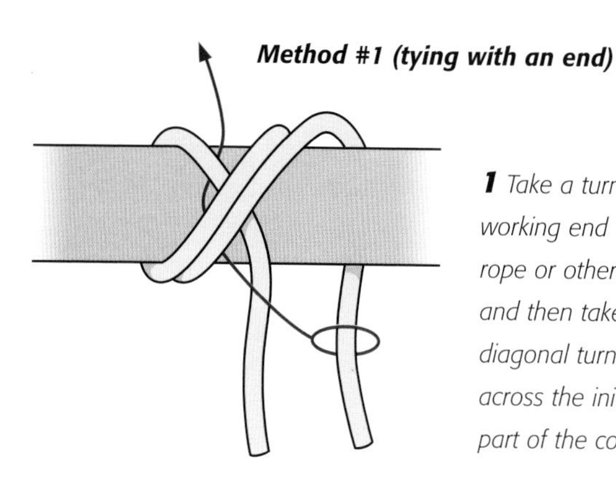

1 *Take a turn with the working end around the rope or other foundation and then take two diagonal turns SW to NE across the initial standing part of the cord.*

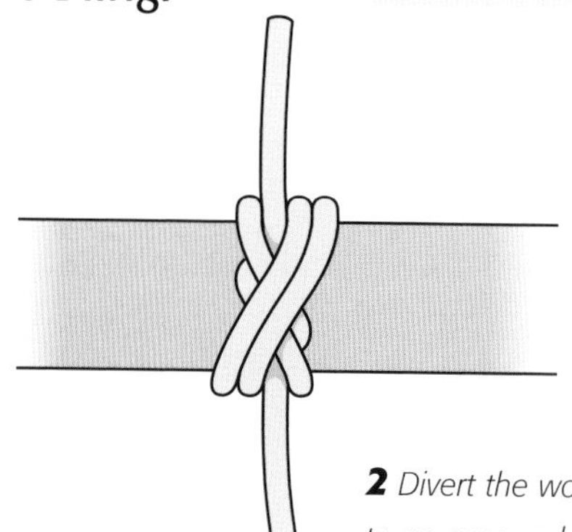

2 *Divert the working end to go over-under-under-under (as shown), before tightening the knot and trimming both ends.*

Method #2 (tying in the bight)

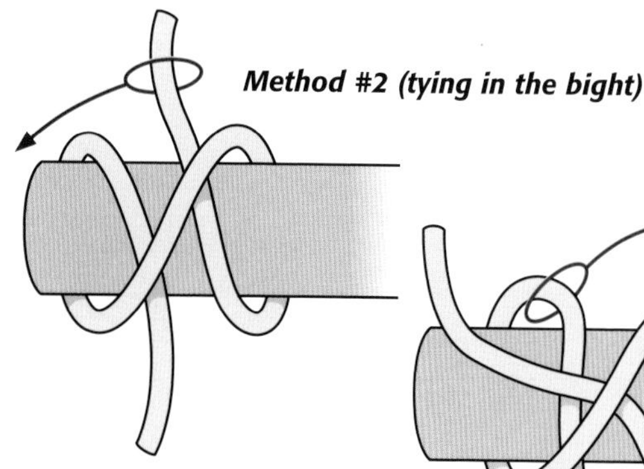

1 *Begin as if tying a letter 'N' (see the preceding constrictor knot), then bring the working end across the knot from right to left.*

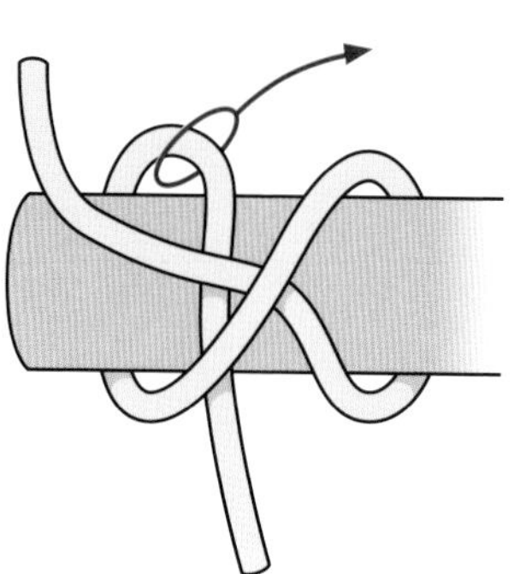

2 *Pull a bight up from the left-hand turn around the foundation.*

3 *Impart half-a-twist to this bight and bring it diagonally downward, from NE to SW, over the end of the foundation.*

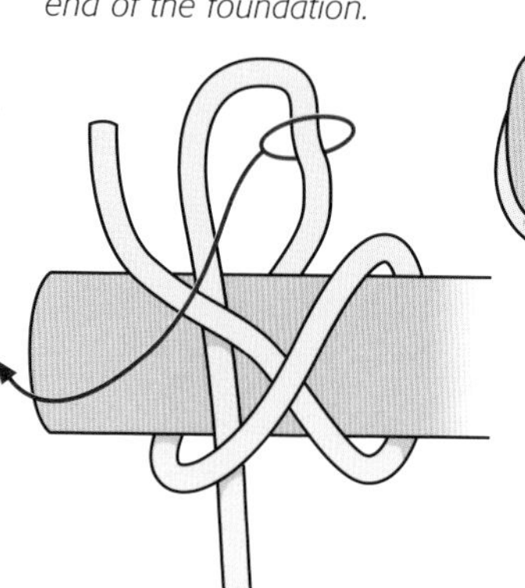

4 *Tighten the completed knot and trim off both ends.*

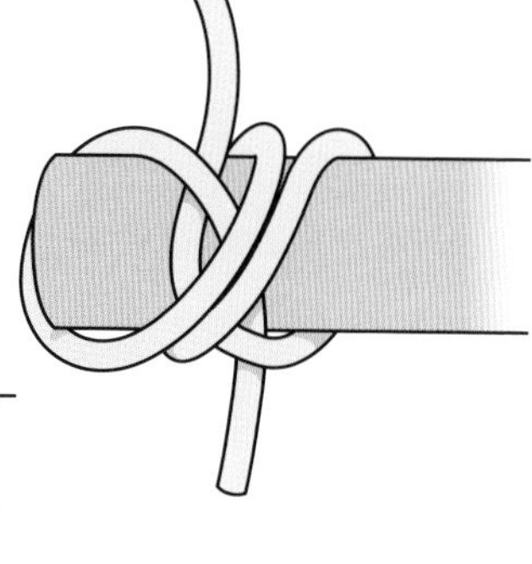

Common whipping

The cut ends of natural fiber cordage cannot be heat-sealed, while tying or taping any cordage (synthetic or natural) should be regarded as only a temporary treatment. Sooner, rather than later, you should apply a whipping.

Expert tip
Use natural fiber whipping twine on natural fiber ropes, and synthetic whipping twine on synthetic ropes.

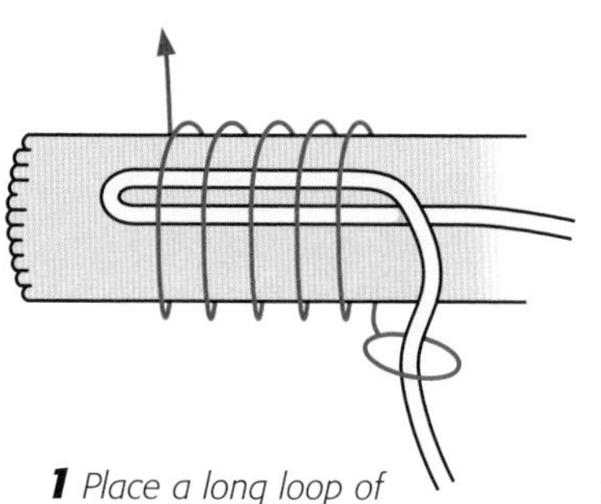

1 *Place a long loop of twine alongside the rope and close to its end.*

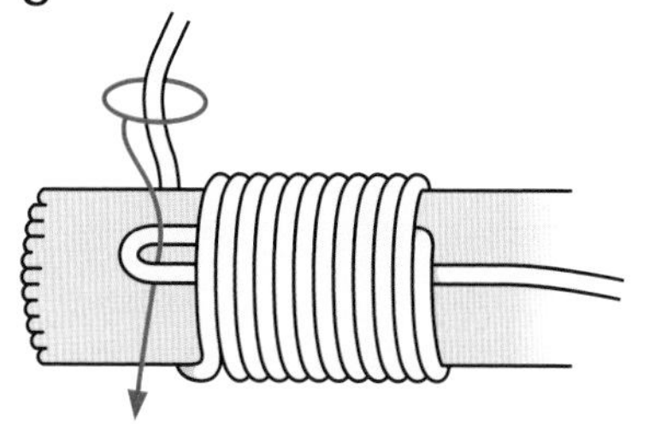

2 *Wrap the working end in a series of tight turns, locating each beside the previous one, until the whipping is at least as wide as the diameter of the rope.*

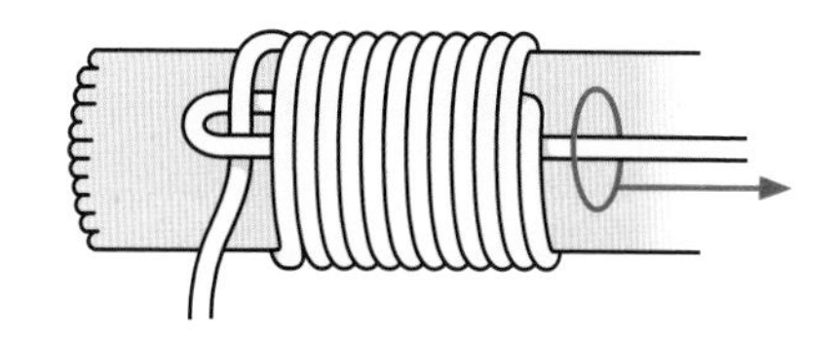

3 *Leave the last turn slightly looser than all of the preceding ones and tuck the working end down through what remains of the initial loop.*

4 *Pull firmly on the standing end, so that the loop retreats beneath the wrapping turns, dragging the working end with it. Stop when the two interlinked elbows of twine are at the center of the whipping. Then neatly trim off both long ends.*

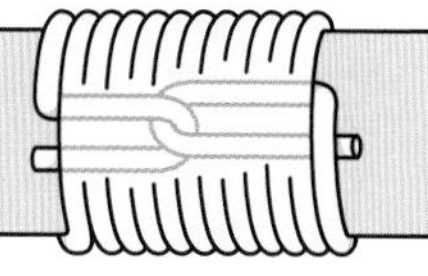

Ashley's stopper knot

When the figure-eight stopper knot (*see page 48*) lacks bulk, and fails to prevent a rope's end from pulling free from a block, fairlead, slot, or other aperture, employ this chunkier stopper.

Knot lore

The renowned knotting author and maritime artist Clifford Ashley discovered this knot over 90 years ago, while drawing and painting scenes of the cultured oyster industry for *Harper's* magazine. This is why those knot tyers who know the story sometimes refer to the knot by the name Ashley used – 'the oysterman's stopper knot.'

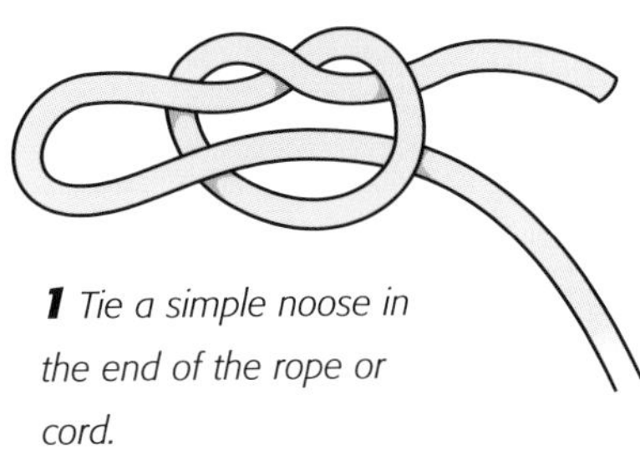

1 *Tie a simple noose in the end of the rope or cord.*

2 *Tighten this slip knot then tuck the working end up through the loop (as shown).*

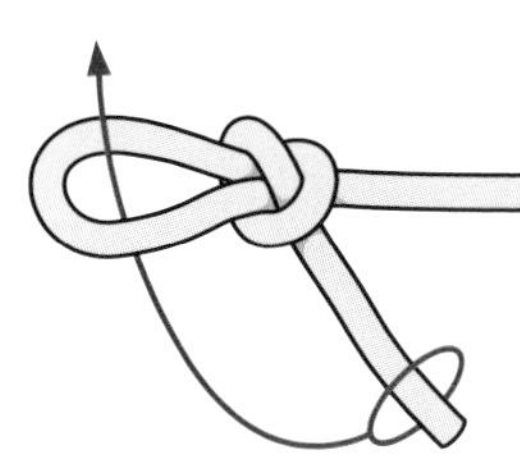

3 *Pull on the standing part of the rope or cord to reduce the loop until it traps and holds the short end.*

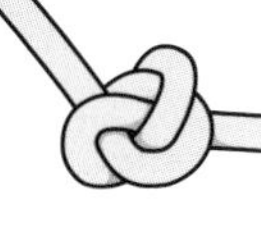

Ossel hitch

Many knots cannot be tied satisfactorily in flat materials, such as tape or webbing, neckties, or bandages. This knot anchors them like superglue sticks to the skin – and it works in round cordage too.

Expert tip

Ensure that the section passing behind the standing part wraps snugly around it like the collar of a jacket.

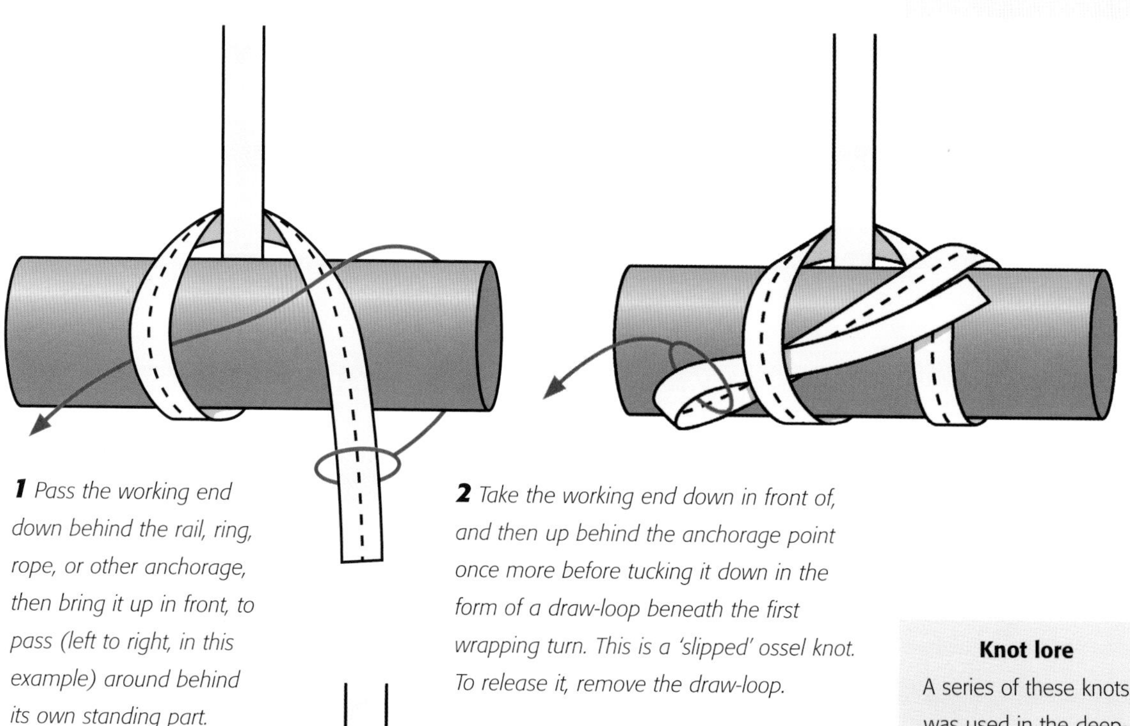

1 *Pass the working end down behind the rail, ring, rope, or other anchorage, then bring it up in front, to pass (left to right, in this example) around behind its own standing part.*

2 *Take the working end down in front of, and then up behind the anchorage point once more before tucking it down in the form of a draw-loop beneath the first wrapping turn. This is a 'slipped' ossel knot. To release it, remove the draw-loop.*

3 *Alternatively, pull the working end completely through the knot for a firmer attachment.*

Knot lore

A series of these knots was used in the deep-sea fishing industry to attach trawl nets to the tow-lines by means of short vertical cords (ossels or norsels) while they were pulled through the water, so it is a very secure hitch.

Hoisting hitch

This rope holdfast will help you to raise sections of drainpipe or guttering aloft; haul felled tree trunks and lopped branches over rough terrain; tow flotsam and salvaged items through water; and, in smaller cordage, it can be employed to haul heavy hand-tools up to elevated work levels where they are required.

Expert tip
Carefully tighten every turn and tuck of this knot, then repeat the process, before loading it.

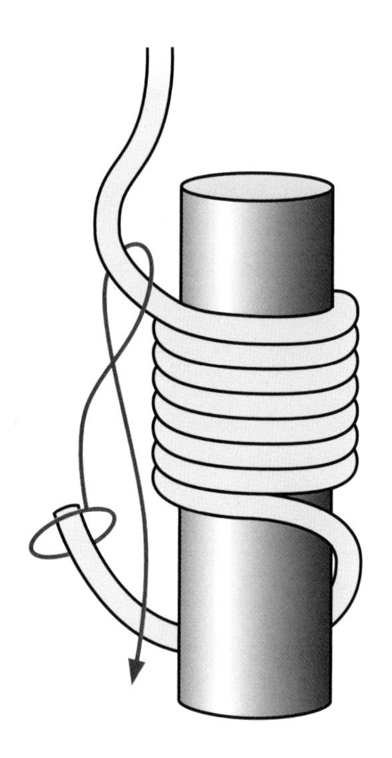

1 *Wrap six to eight turns, working away from the end of the object to be lifted.*

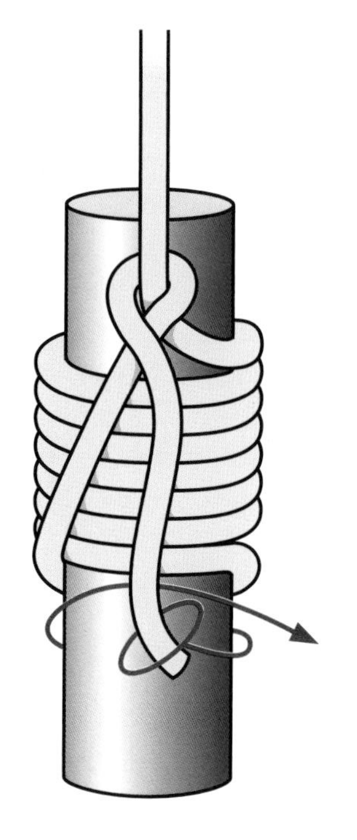

2 *Bring the working end diagonally upward (in this instance, from SW to NE) and take it around behind the standing part of the rope or cord (from right to left).*

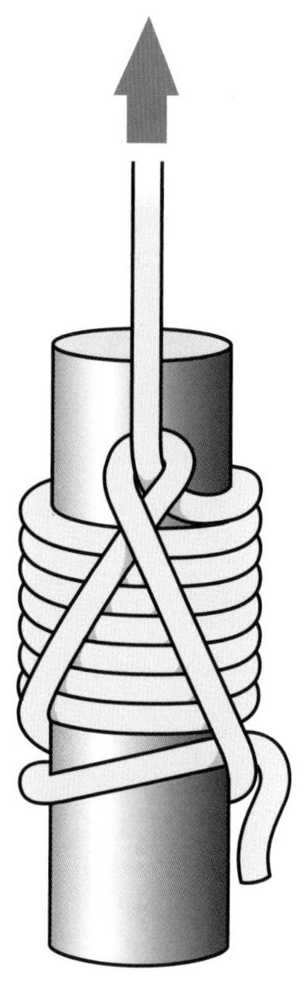

3 *Finally, take a turn with the working end and lock it off with a half-hitch.*

Above: *Health and safely at workplaces like this construction site depend upon avoiding foreseeable hazards. The hoisting hitch, carefully applied, is a reliable cordage contrivance.*

Asher's bottle sling

A bottle sling enables you to lug around the heaviest bottles, flasks and flagons, jars or jugs, containing all kinds of liquid and liquor (from drinking water to battery acid). Or you can suspend bottled beverages in a cooling stream prior to a summer picnic.

Expert tip

Just as for the hoisting hitch (already described), carefully tighten every turn and tuck of this knot, then repeat the process, before putting it to use.

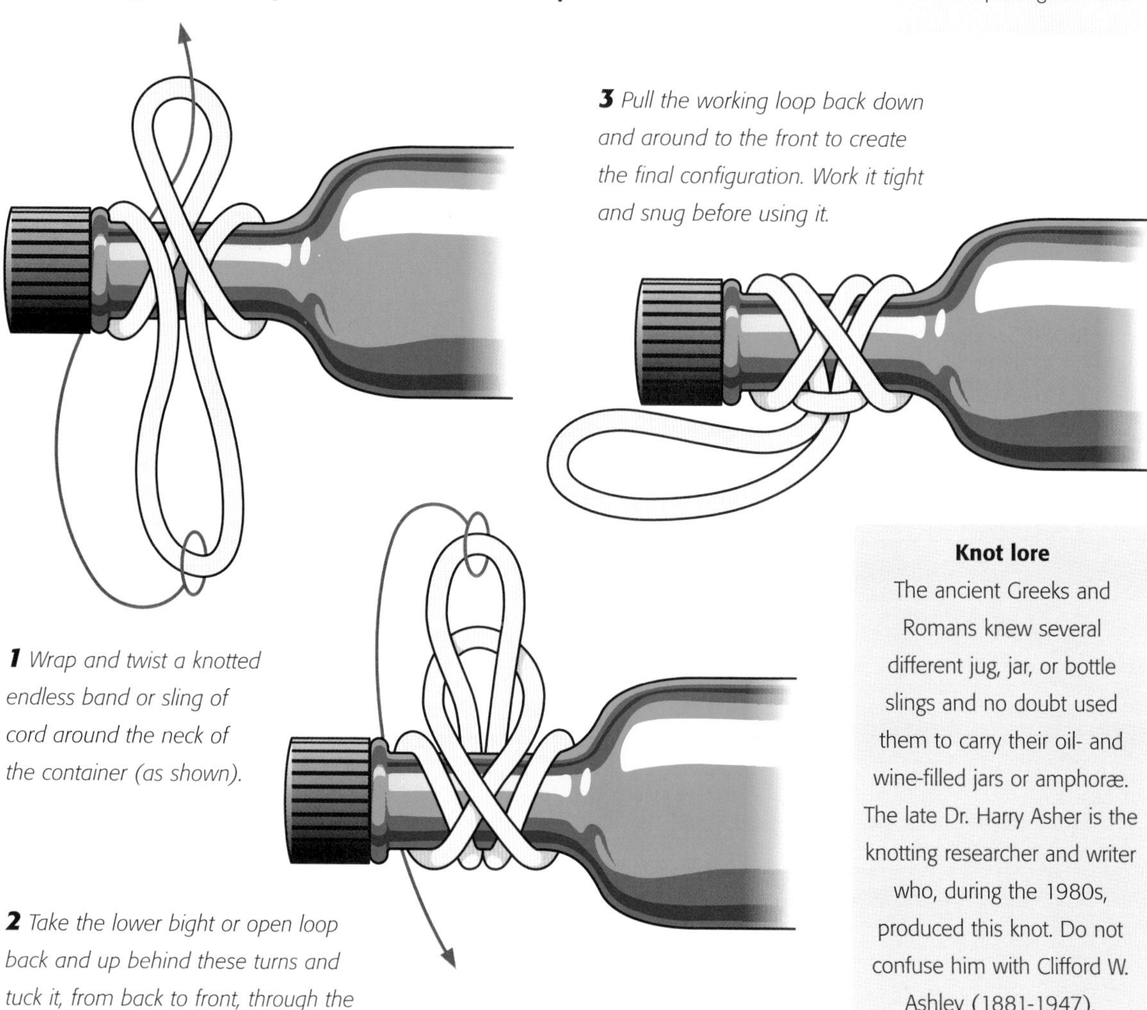

1 *Wrap and twist a knotted endless band or sling of cord around the neck of the container (as shown).*

2 *Take the lower bight or open loop back and up behind these turns and tuck it, from back to front, through the crossed upper loop.*

3 *Pull the working loop back down and around to the front to create the final configuration. Work it tight and snug before using it.*

Knot lore

The ancient Greeks and Romans knew several different jug, jar, or bottle slings and no doubt used them to carry their oil- and wine-filled jars or amphoræ. The late Dr. Harry Asher is the knotting researcher and writer who, during the 1980s, produced this knot. Do not confuse him with Clifford W. Ashley (1881-1947).

Perfection loop

When a bowline (*see page 60*) is likely to slip and spill – for instance, in hard-laid synthetics – use this more secure fixed loop knot. It will even hold in shock elastics (bungee cords), which shrug off many other knots, and can be made in thin string to tie up a parcel.

Knot lore
In the days before nylon monofilaments, when anglers relied upon fishing lines made from horsehair, gut, or silk, the perfection loop began many a tackle rig. For this reason it is still widely known by its other name – the angler's loop.

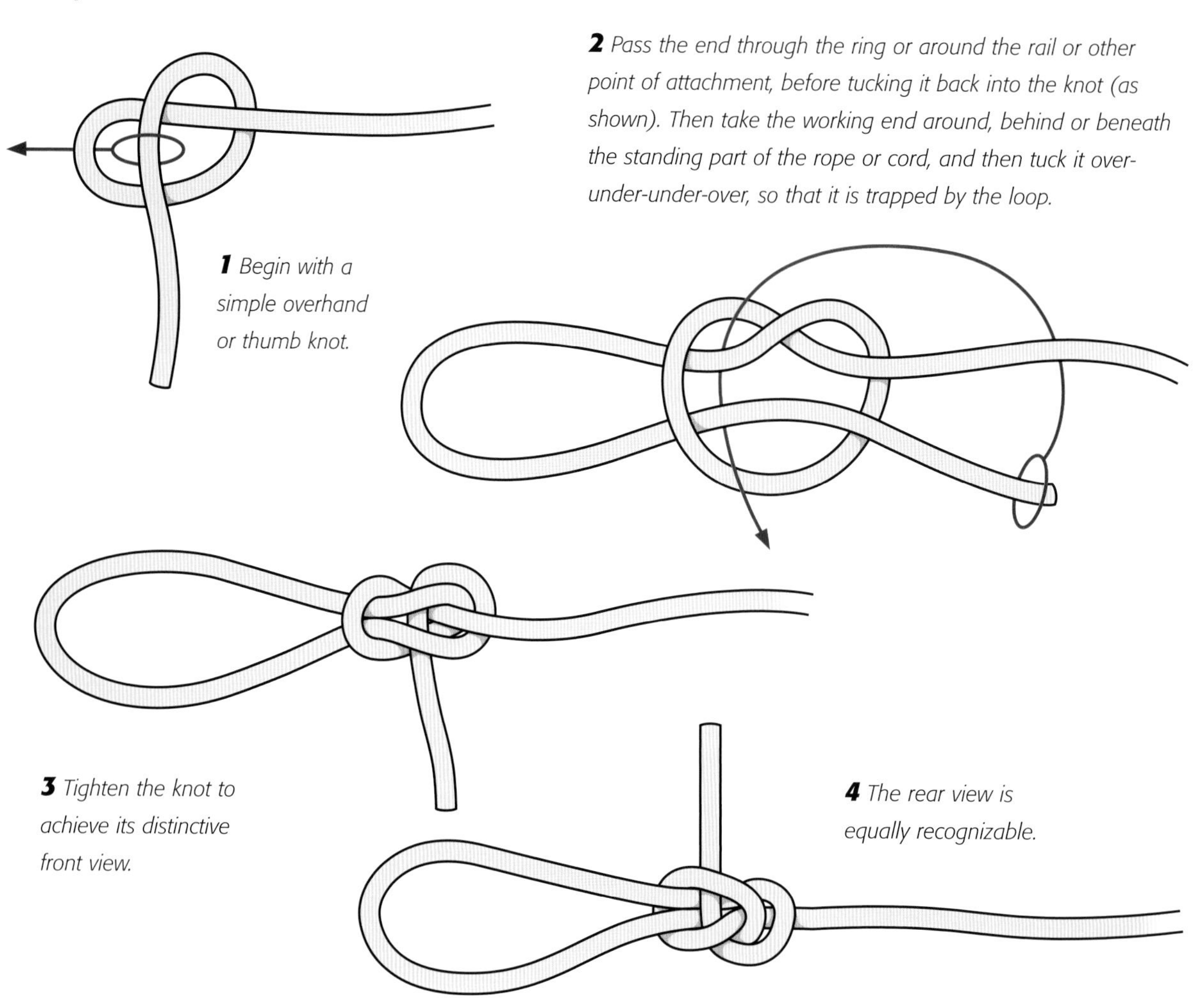

1 *Begin with a simple overhand or thumb knot.*

2 *Pass the end through the ring or around the rail or other point of attachment, before tucking it back into the knot (as shown). Then take the working end around, behind or beneath the standing part of the rope or cord, and then tuck it over-under-under-over, so that it is trapped by the loop.*

3 *Tighten the knot to achieve its distinctive front view.*

4 *The rear view is equally recognizable.*

Tarbuck knot

This slide-and-grip loop knot or noose is ideal for guy-lines on tents and marquees or patio awnings, and for other types of stays and shrouds (for instance, to brace a windbreak on the beach at the seaside), which may from time to time need to be adjusted.

Expert tip

Grasp the knot and slide it along until the loop is the required size. When loaded, it will hold firm by creating a dog's leg deformation in the standing part of the line. Remove the load and it can be readjusted.

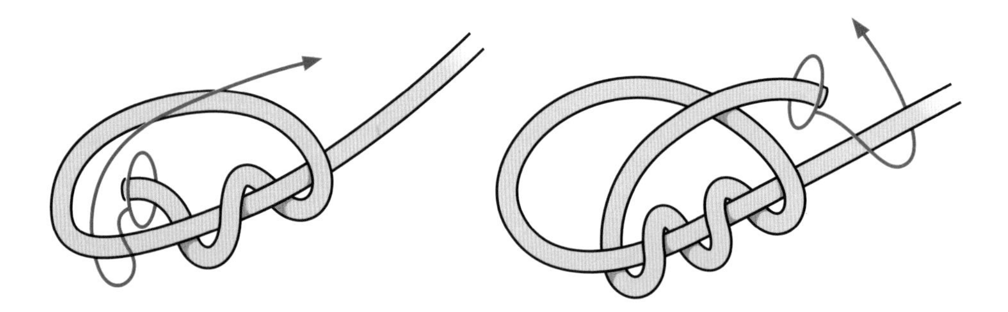

1 *Form an overhand loop and then tuck the working end twice through and around itself (as shown).*

2 *Next, take the working end up and around behind the standing part of the line from right to left.*

Knot lore

This knot was known and used by American tree surgeons (who called it 'the squeeze knot') in Wisconsin during the 1940s; but it was popularized in the UK during the 1950s by British climbing writer Ken Tarbuck – after whom it is named – to cope with the new-fangled hawser-laid nylon climbing ropes. It soon proved to be unsuitable, however, for sheath-and-core (kernmantel) cordage, and so is now only recommended for use as a general-purpose loop knot.

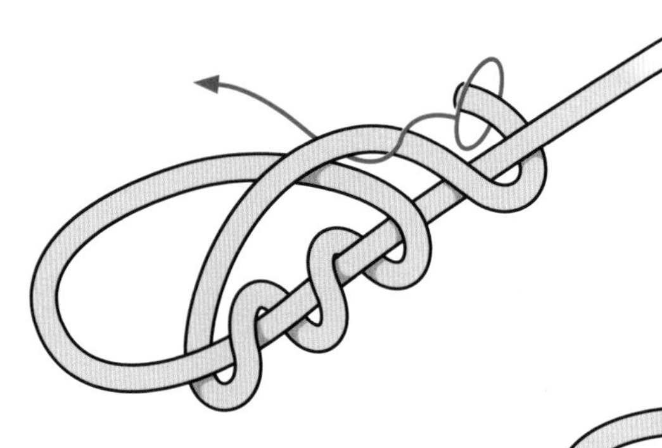

3 *Then tuck the end over and down through the loop just made.*

4 *Tighten all the wrapping turns and the final locking tuck with care before loading the knot.*

Sister loops

This curious cordage contrivance has no known role, but it can come in handy for all sorts of purposes: to catch a stray animal; to lift and carry one's home computer to the repair shop; to improvise reins and so safeguard a toddler in a crowded shopping mall. The possibilities are as endless as the twin fixed loops.

Knot lore

This device is featured by the Australian knotting writer Charles Warner in his 1992 book *A Fresh Approach to Knotting and Ropework*. The knot is an odd maverick and the name used here is the one he assigns to it.

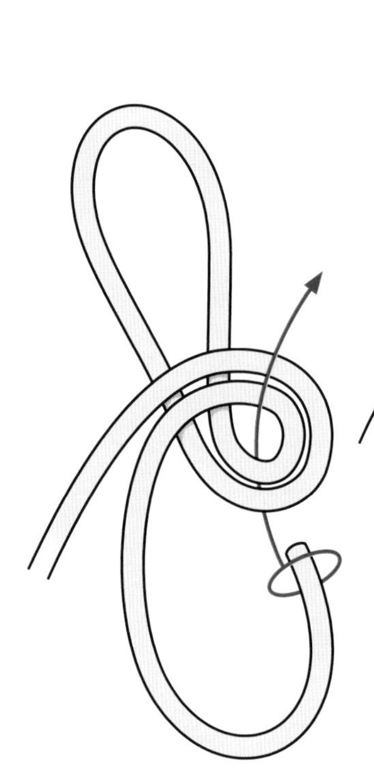

1 *Make a bight in a length of cord and cast a small doubled underhand loop in it, at the same time creating a larger single loop.*

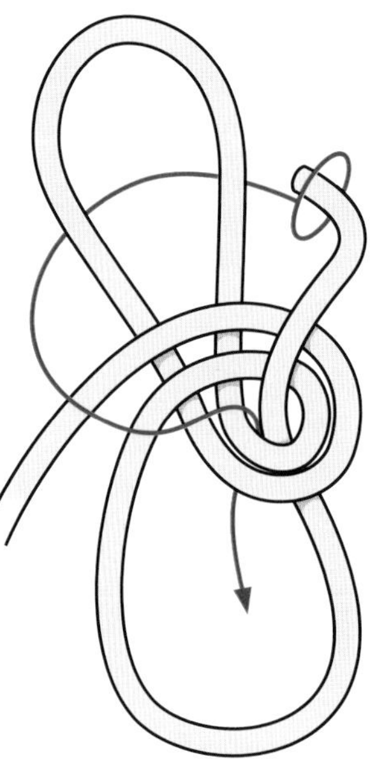

2 *Leaving the shorter end alone, lead the longer end around to form a matching second single loop, and tuck the end up through the small doubled loops.*

3 *Take the working end around behind the upper single loop and then bring it forward and down through the doubled loops.*

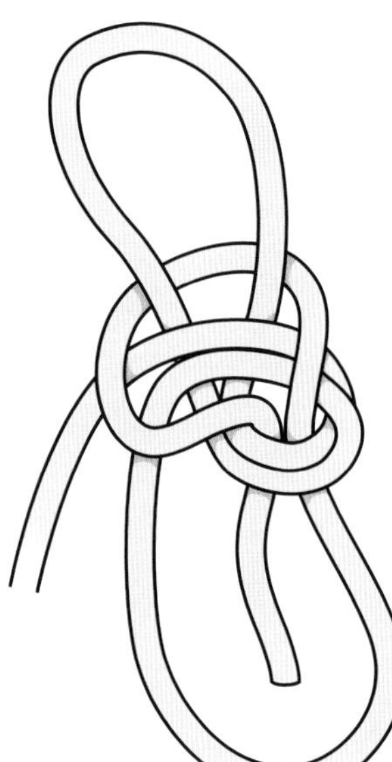

4 *Adjust the twin single loops to the required size, then tighten the entire knot and trim both ends.*

Sheepshank

This underrated knot is, in fact, quite versatile. It can shorten a rope or long cord without cutting it, and so preserve it intact for re-use another time; or it will, temporarily, bridge a damaged and weakened section of a rope until it can be replaced. A rudimentary sheepshank suspends bell ropes tidily and safely in a church belfry when not required, and the same knot forms the cordage purchase, applied in bygone days by carters to lash down loads securely, known today as the trucker's hitch.

Knot lore

It is most unlikely that this knot was ever used to tether sheep while they grazed; but it may be that the knot was named for its resemblance to one of that creature's leg bones.

Weak or damaged section.

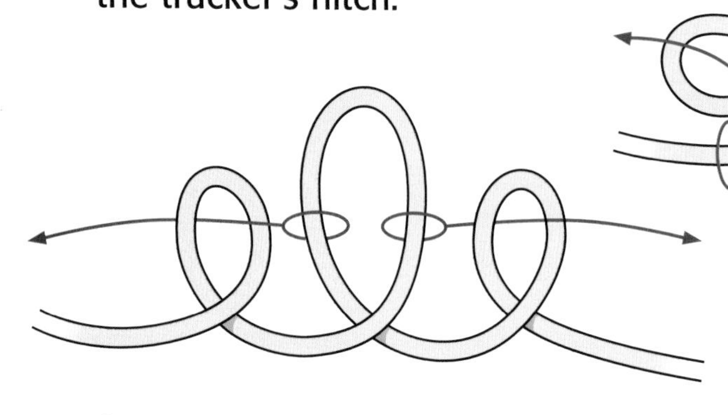

2 *Pull the left-hand leg of the central loop out through the nearest smaller loop, going over-under. Similarly, pull the right-hand loop leg out through its adjacent smaller loop, going under-over (as pictured above).*

1 *Cast a trio of loops – two of them overhand, the third underhand – with the middle one bigger than the others.*

3 *Finally lock off the end loops in one of two ways: either pull the standing part of the line right the way through, creating a layout similar to that of the bowline (see page 60); or trap the standing part against the end loop with an improvised toggle that could be a length of wooden doweling, a screwdriver, a spanner, or anything else of the right size and rigidity.*

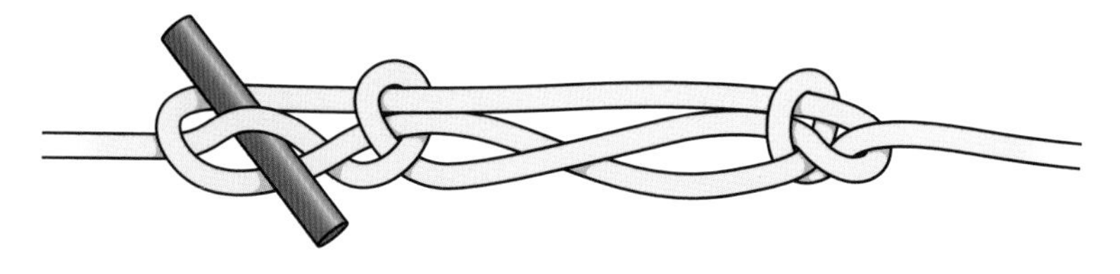

Chinese cross knot

This gathering knot holds two strands together and could embellish a lanyard from which is suspended a sports coach's stopwatch, a referee's whistle, or a lucky amulet. It also works well as a chic neckscarf knot, neatly filling the V-shaped open neck of a blouse or shirt.

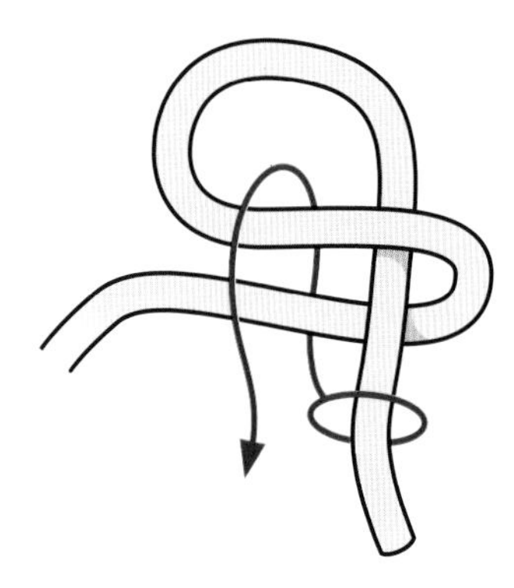

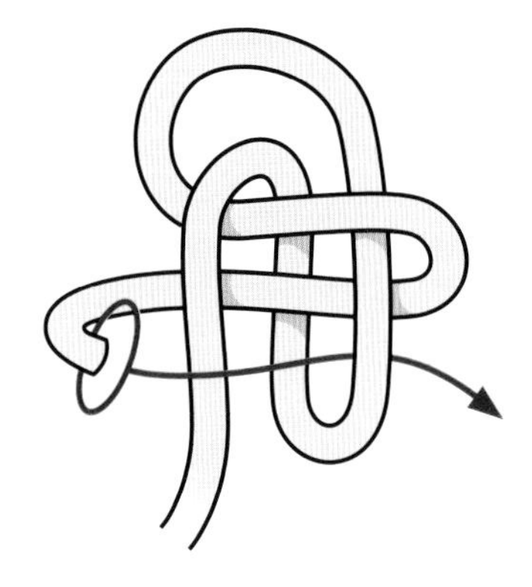

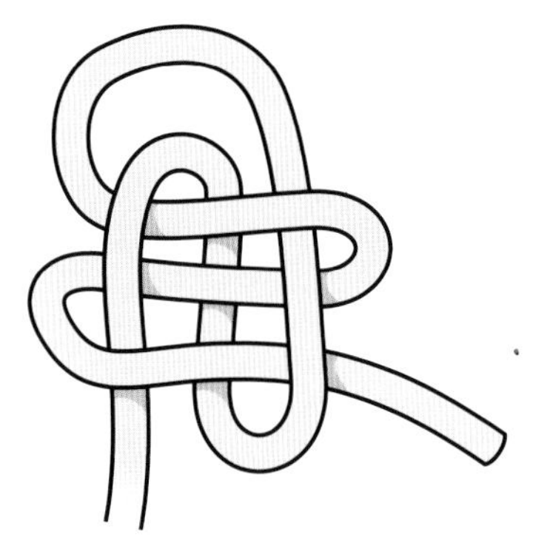

1 *First make a lanyard loop, or pass a scarf around the wearer's neck, then form a bight in one end so that it encloses the other end.*

2 *Tuck the second end up behind the initial bight, then bring it over and down in front once more.*

3 *Pick up the first end and make a locking tuck (as shown).*

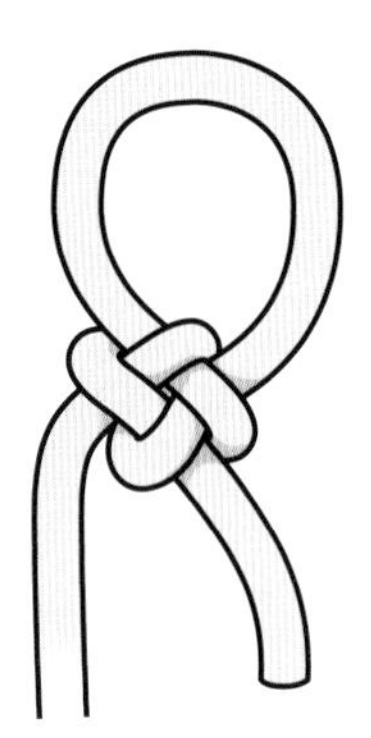

4 *Tighten the knot to display the regular four-part crown face.*

5 *The rear of this knot is equally distinctive but less decorative.*

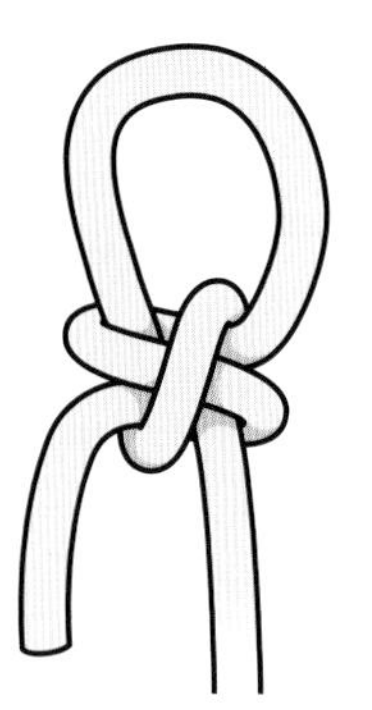

Knot lore

A simple cross in Chinese represents 'ten,' and what Westerners regard as its decorative face may – in China – be the back of the knot, hence its Oriental name 'cross knot.'

Braid knot

Expert tip
It is unlikely that this braid will be completely snug and firm when first tied. Starting at one end, pull any remaining slack through the knot, from one end to the other, then back again (in a bight of increasing size), then a third time through the knot until all of the slack can be pulled away by the other end.

This neat and natty bit of knotting will serve to embellish a light-pull or curtain tie-back; it can act as a get-you-home replacement for a broken suitcase handle; or simply help to shorten a needlessly long piece of line.

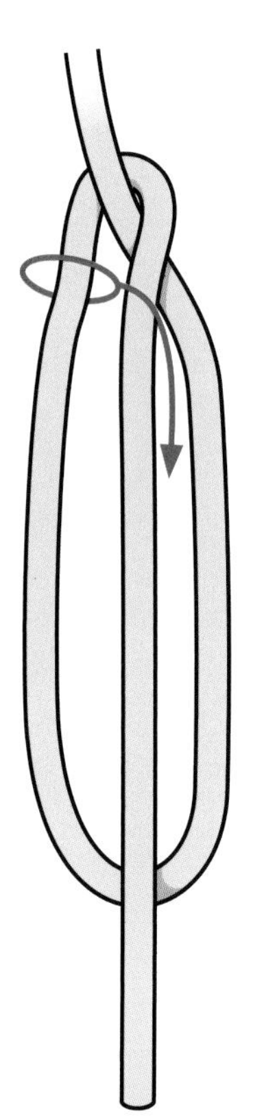

1 *Create a long loop so that the cord is arranged in three parts.*

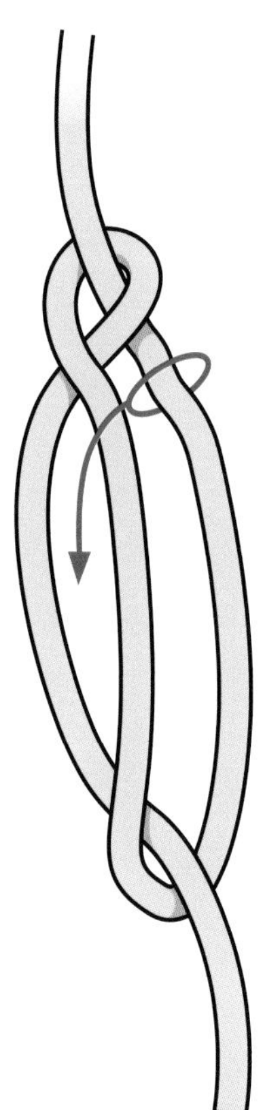

2 *Begin to make a three-strand plait, left-over-middle, right-over-middle.*

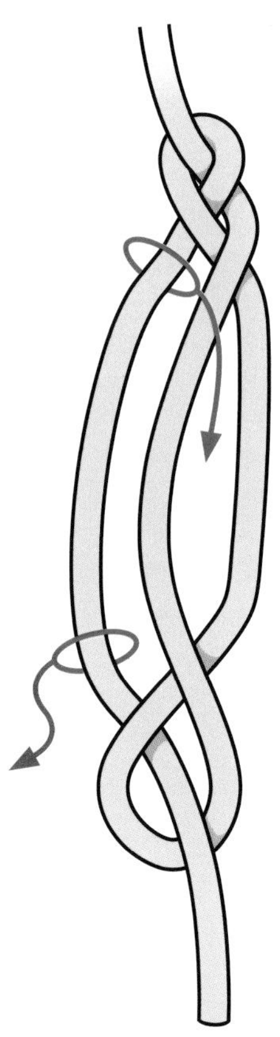

3 *At intervals, untangle the long end from the bottom of the emerging plait.*

4 *When the entire loop is plaited, make one final locking tuck.*

BOATING KNOTS

Never venture out on water without various bits and pieces of cordage. It may seem as if the fixtures and fittings and rigging terminals found aboard contemporary boats make knotting unnecessary, but however you go afloat – in a superyacht or sailing dinghy, a gin palace of a motor cruiser, a canal boat or a canoe, riding a windsurfer or straddling a jet-bike – the time will come (more often than not, it seems, on a Spring ebb tide) when your safety and convenience depend upon the rapid recall of some knots.

All boating knots must be relatively strong and secure – but quickly cast off when necessary – and the selection that follows in this section all have those qualities.

Figure-eight stopper knot

Any ropes rove through fairleads or blocks – such as jib leads and main sheets, and perhaps halyards too – should have stopper knots tied in their ends to prevent them from pulling free. This knot is usually best for that kind of job.

Expert tip

If the figure-eight knot is not large enough to retain the line in whatever ought to hold it, then use Ashley's stopper knot (*see page 27*).

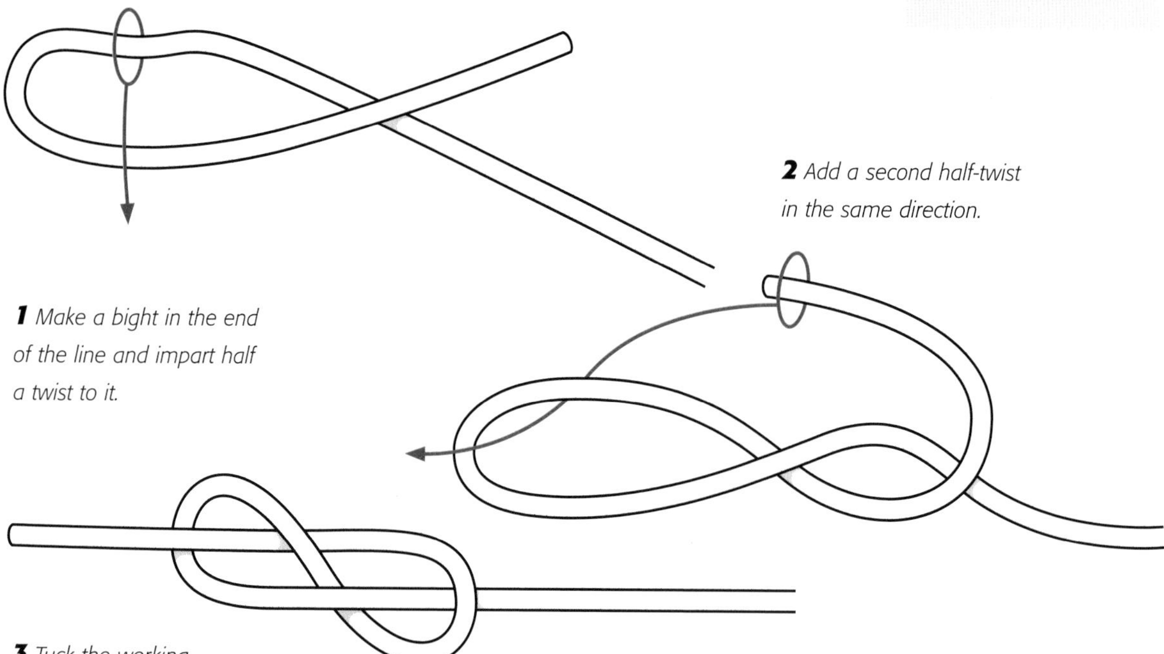

__1__ Make a bight in the end of the line and impart half a twist to it.

__2__ Add a second half-twist in the same direction.

__3__ Tuck the working end through to complete the knot.

__4__ Tighten the knot by holding it and pulling on the standing part so as to wrap and trap the short end more or less at a right-angle to the rest of the rope.

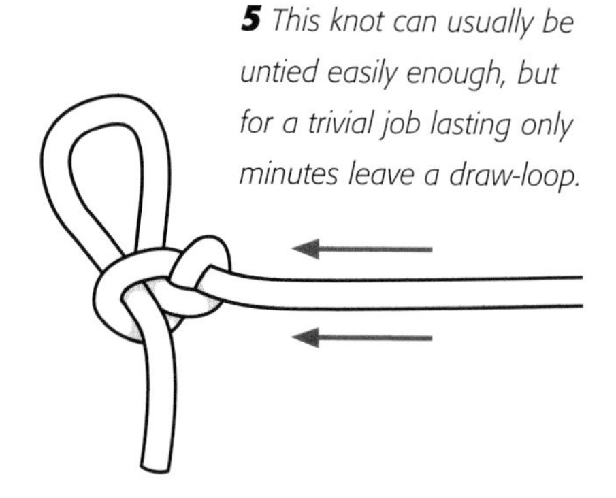

__5__ This knot can usually be untied easily enough, but for a trivial job lasting only minutes leave a draw-loop.

Knot lore

This knot is occasionally still referred to by its much older name – 'Flemish knot.'

Round turn and two half-hitches

Below: *Boats are not simply parked – but must be tied up with bowlines (or painters) and stern lines, and perhaps with springs and breast ropes too.*

This go-anywhere, do-anything knot will attach most kinds of cordage to a rail, ring, spar, post, or another rope, and withstand a pull that is steady or intermittent and from various directions. Employ it when anchoring, mooring, or berthing; to belay a safety harness or other tether to a fixed point; to suspend fenders outboard; and to tow a dinghy astern.

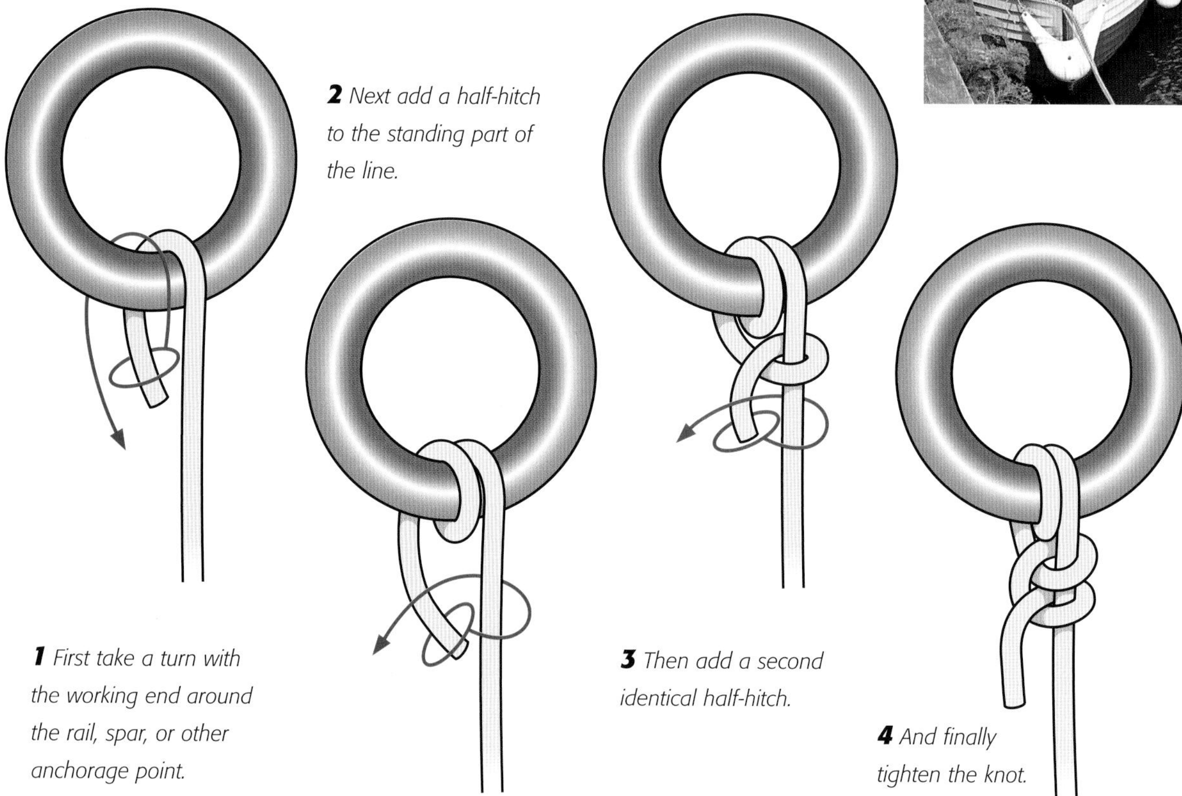

1 *First take a turn with the working end around the rail, spar, or other anchorage point.*

2 *Next add a half-hitch to the standing part of the line.*

3 *Then add a second identical half-hitch.*

4 *And finally tighten the knot.*

Fisherman's bend

When the preceding round turn and two half-hitches is likely to become wet and slippery, or for any other reason less reliable, resort to this more secure variant of that knot.

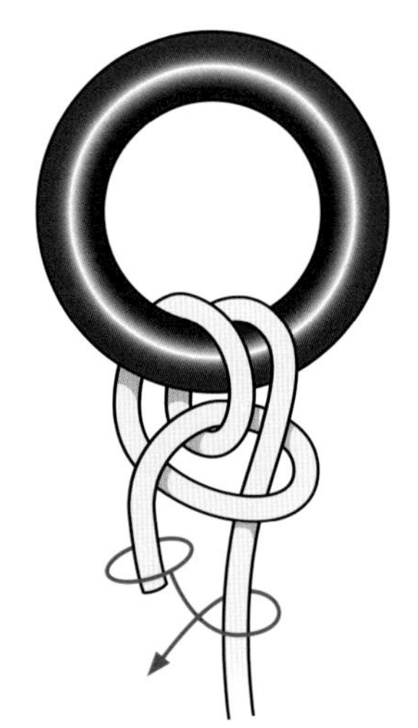

***1** Take a turn with the working end around the ring and then insert a half-hitch through that turn before tying it around the standing part of the line.*

***2** Add a second identical half-hitch and tighten the knot.*

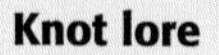

Knot lore

The fisherman's bend is traditionally recommended for attaching rope warps to the rings of small anchors. It is, of course, really a hitch, and its appellation 'bend' results from the fact that, in an earlier epoch, sailors spoke of 'bending' a rope to a ring.

Figure-eight becket hitch

To attach a line to an eye, or the permanent seized loops known as beckets, use this simplest of hitches.

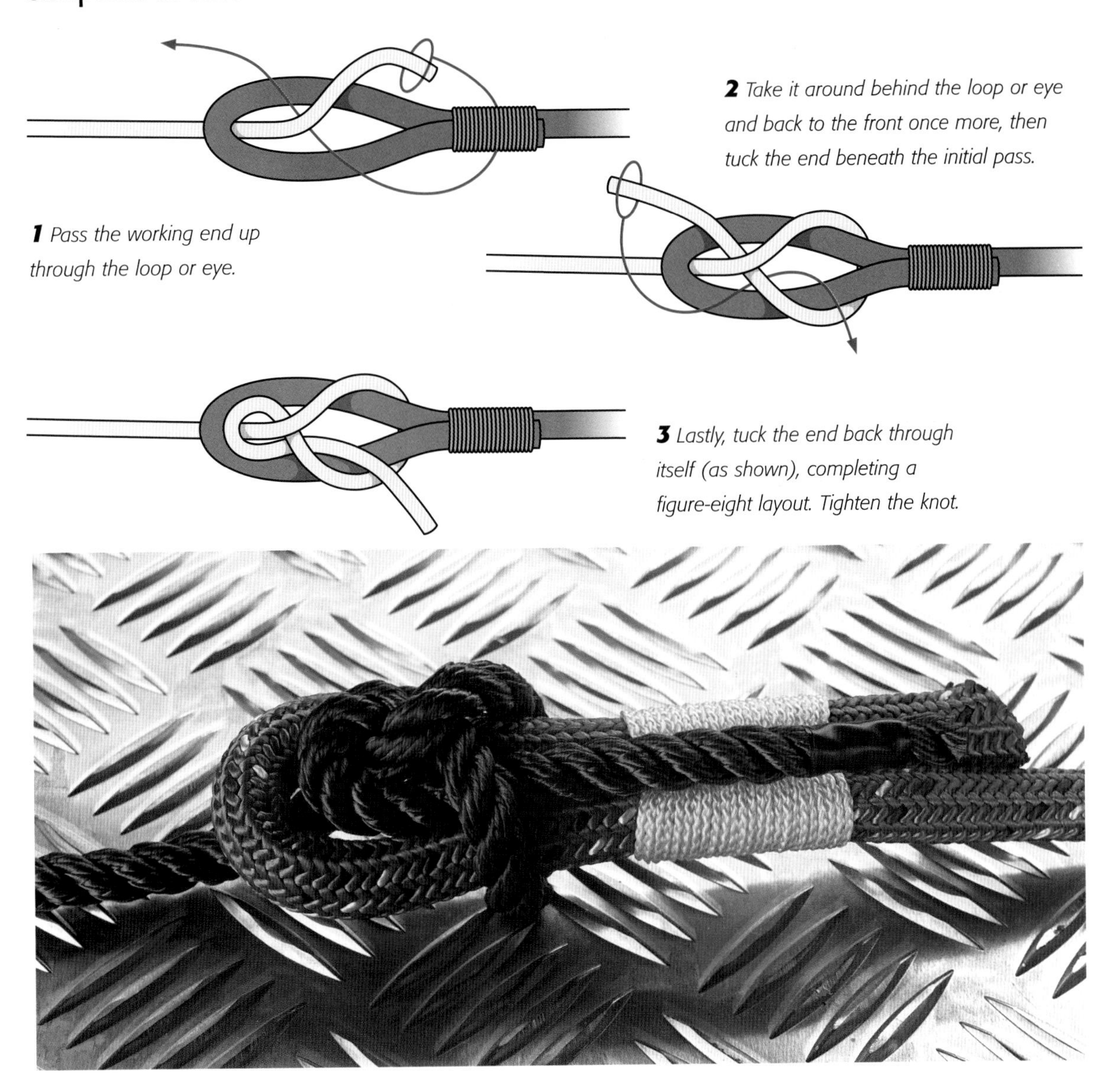

1 *Pass the working end up through the loop or eye.*

2 *Take it around behind the loop or eye and back to the front once more, then tuck the end beneath the initial pass.*

3 *Lastly, tuck the end back through itself (as shown), completing a figure-eight layout. Tighten the knot.*

Ossel knot

Unlike the ossel hitch (*see page 28*), with which it should not be confused, this knot is unsuitable for webbing. But, in cordage, it is tougher and more tenacious than its less robust relative, and will cope with a pull that varies in direction.

Knot lore
Like the ossel hitch, this knot was employed in the sea fishing industry to secure trawl nets to their towing lines, but it was used closer to the surface where the water was rougher. As it survived being dragged along and yanked around in such conditions, it is a tried-and-trusted knot.

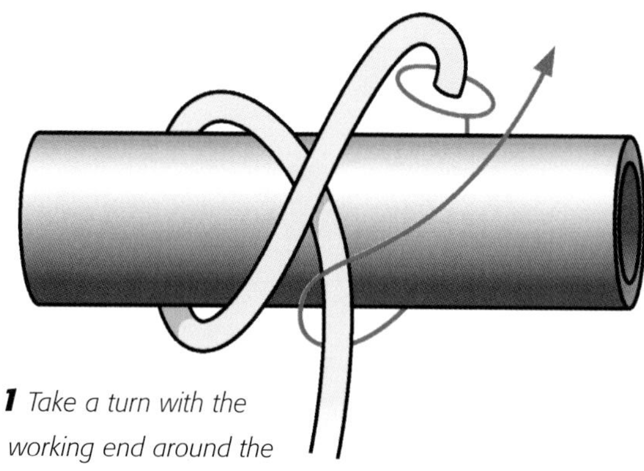

1 *Take a turn with the working end around the foundation, to the left of the standing part of the line (in this instance), and then create a diagonal that crosses SW to NE, wrapping and trapping the standing part.*

2 *Then take the end around a second time to create another similar diagonal, alongside and below the first one.*

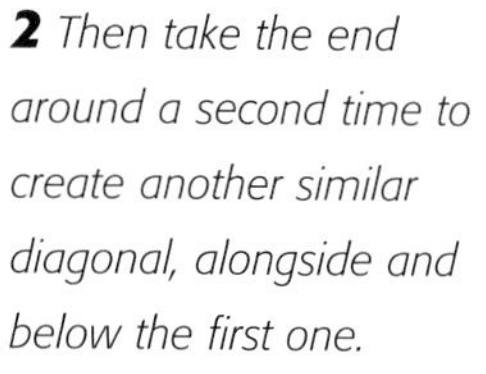

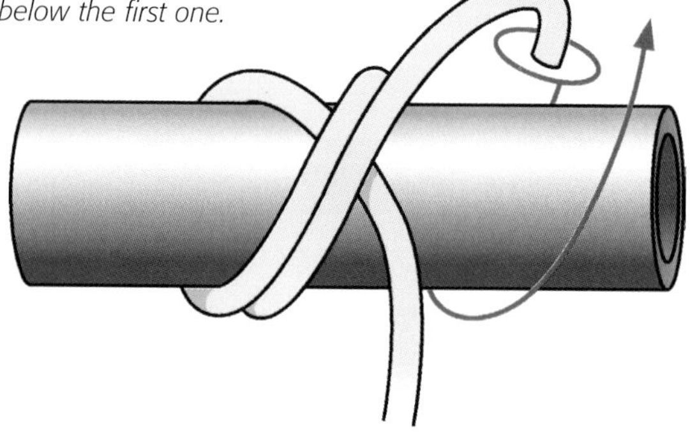

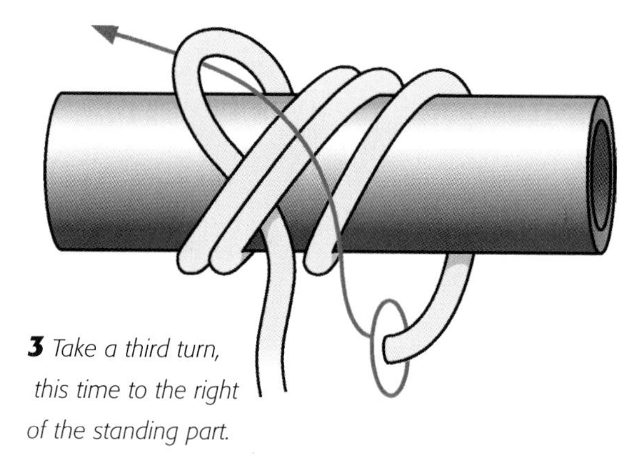

3 *Take a third turn, this time to the right of the standing part.*

4 *Lastly, tuck the working end, going SE to NW, over-over-over-under, and work the knot tight.*

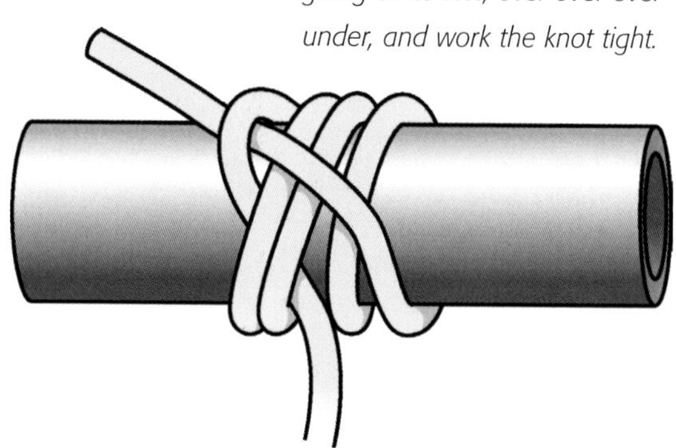

Boom hitch

Expert tip
To tie this knot, and do it right, repeat the mantra; 'Over – over – over – over – and tuck'.

This handsome and semi-permanent hitch can be tied in webbing or cordage. Use it when strength, security, and style are desirable.

Knot lore
When the main sheet broke free from the boom of my sailing dinghy, I reattached it with a lanyard and this knot. Then, not only was I able to beat back against wind and tide to causeway, car, and trailer, but I left it in place and used it for the rest of the summer boating season.

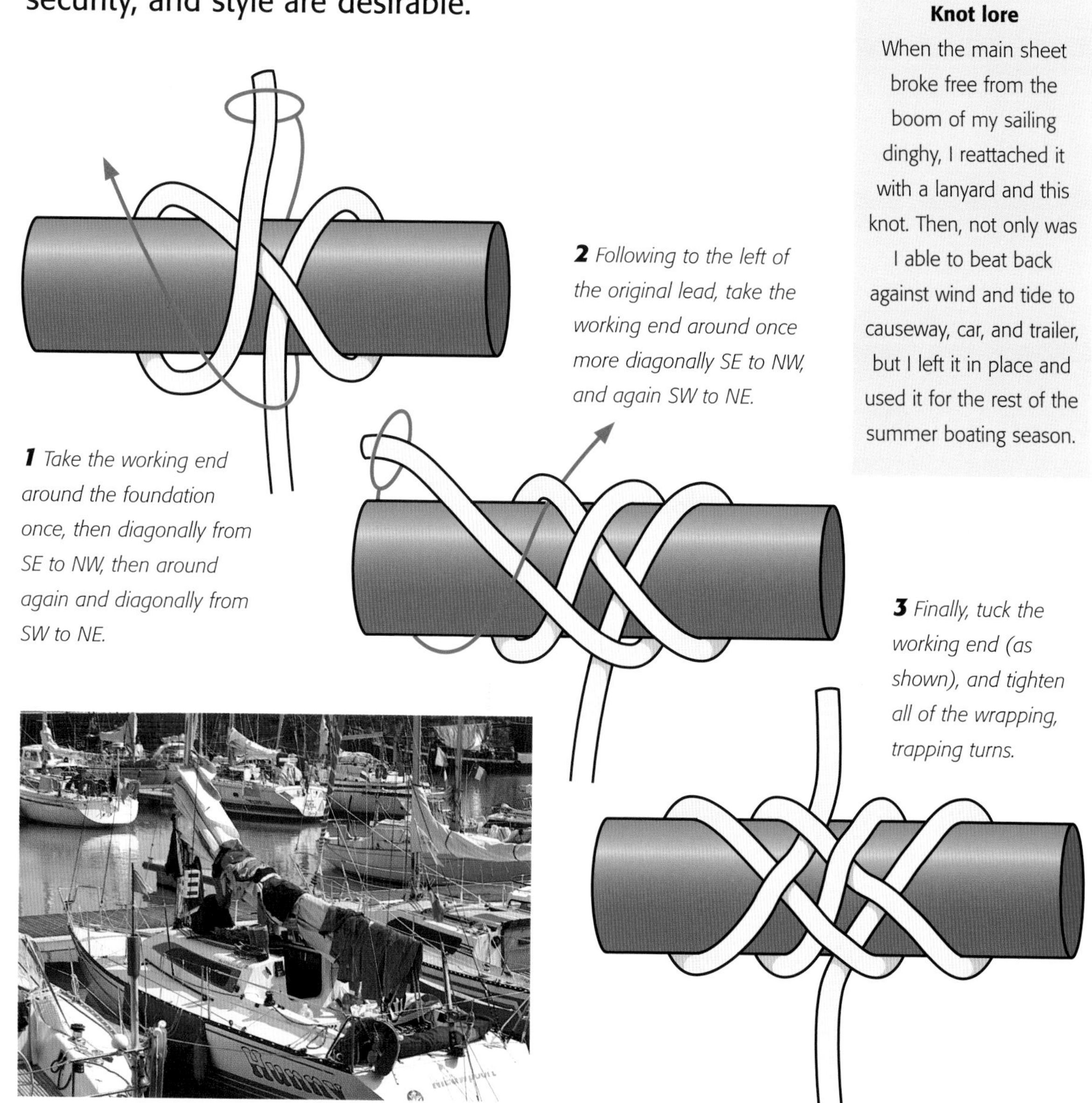

__1__ Take the working end around the foundation once, then diagonally from SE to NW, then around again and diagonally from SW to NE.

__2__ Following to the left of the original lead, take the working end around once more diagonally SE to NW, and again SW to NE.

__3__ Finally, tuck the working end (as shown), and tighten all of the wrapping, trapping turns.

Pile hitch

A series of these hitches can be used ashore to secure a barrier rope to a row of vertical posts or stakes. Afloat it is a useful way to tie up small craft for a short stay in harbor or alongside a river or canal bank. The pile hitch is also a handy way to improvise T-shaped handles with which to heave on the ends of binding knots such as the constrictor and double constrictor (*see pages 22–25*) to tighten them more than could possibly be done by hand alone.

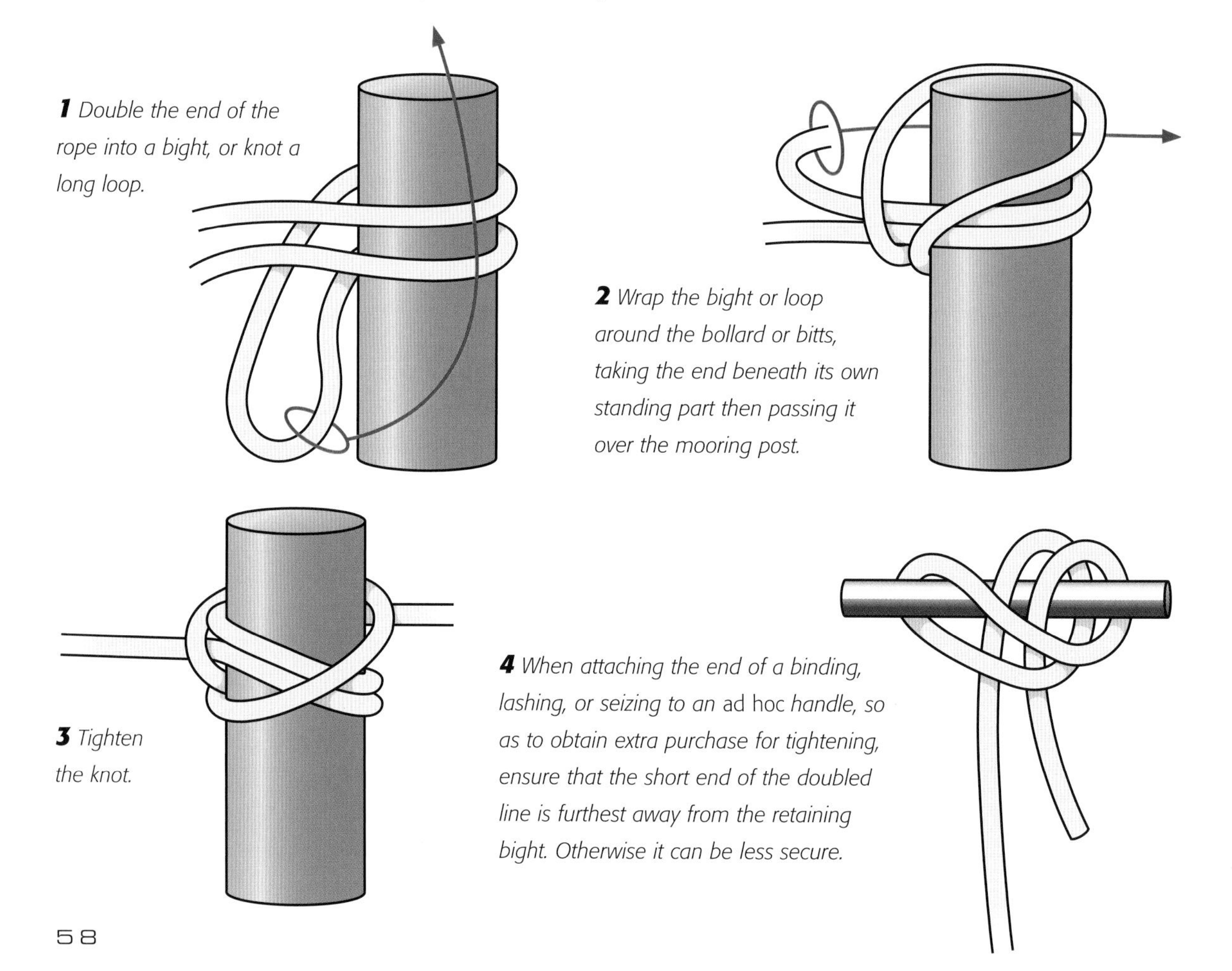

1 *Double the end of the rope into a bight, or knot a long loop.*

2 *Wrap the bight or loop around the bollard or bitts, taking the end beneath its own standing part then passing it over the mooring post.*

3 *Tighten the knot.*

4 *When attaching the end of a binding, lashing, or seizing to an* ad hoc *handle, so as to obtain extra purchase for tightening, ensure that the short end of the doubled line is furthest away from the retaining bight. Otherwise it can be less secure.*

 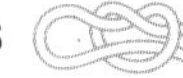

Bowline

(pronounced 'boh-linn')

This is the fixed loop of first choice afloat for attaching a line to a ring or eye. It is also recommended for dropping over a mooring post or bollard, when it serves as a hitch … a hitch, moreover, that can be used, removed, and reused without the need to untie and retie it.

Expert tip
Despite this knot's sobriquet 'King of Knots,' there are stronger and more secure fixed loops; but it is dependable enough, while the ease with which it can be tied, untied, and cast off in crucial seconds have kept it in the repertoire of boating knots for several centuries.

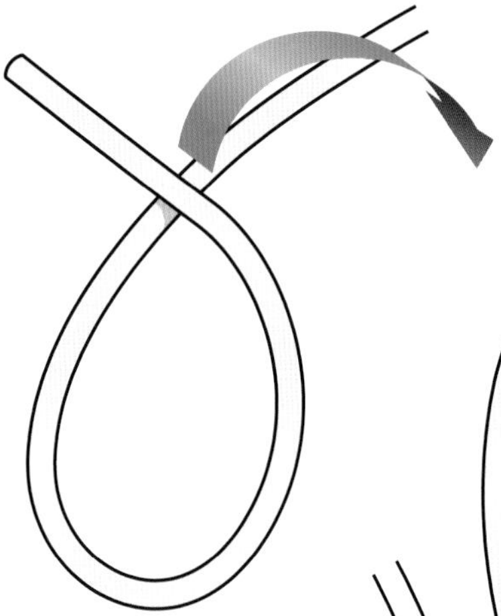

***1** Make an overhand loop and grip it firmly in the right hand (thumb underneath, fingers on top).*

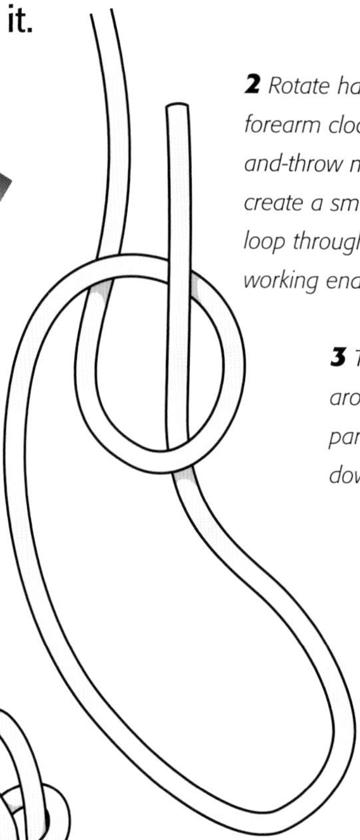

***2** Rotate hand and forearm clockwise, in a trip-and-throw movement, to create a smaller secondary loop through which the working end projects.*

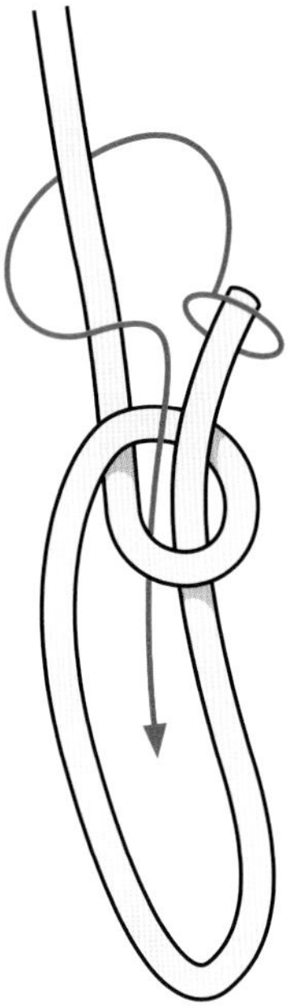

***3** Then take the working end around behind the standing part of the line and tuck it down through the small loop.*

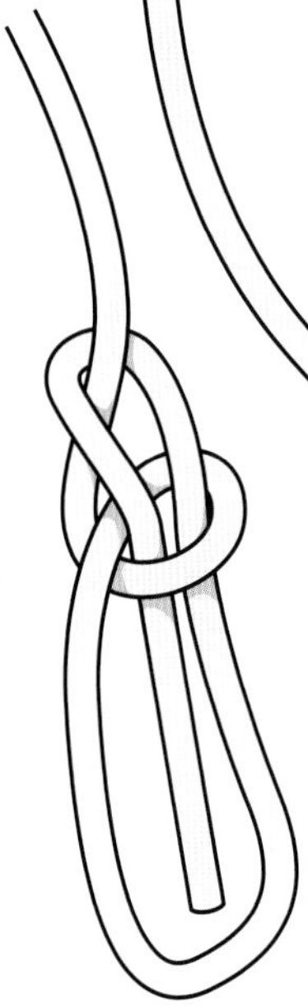

***4** Adjust the main loop to the required size and ensure that the end is almost as long as the adjacent loop leg.*

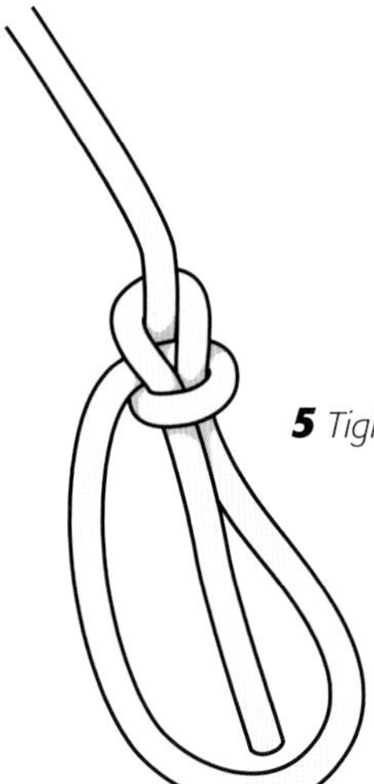

***5** Tighten the knot.*

Scaffold knot

When a loop knot is employed as a hitch, and that hitch must grip firmly around its belay, use this noose. It also works well as a 'hard eye' (that is, an eye reinforced with a plastic or metal thimble).

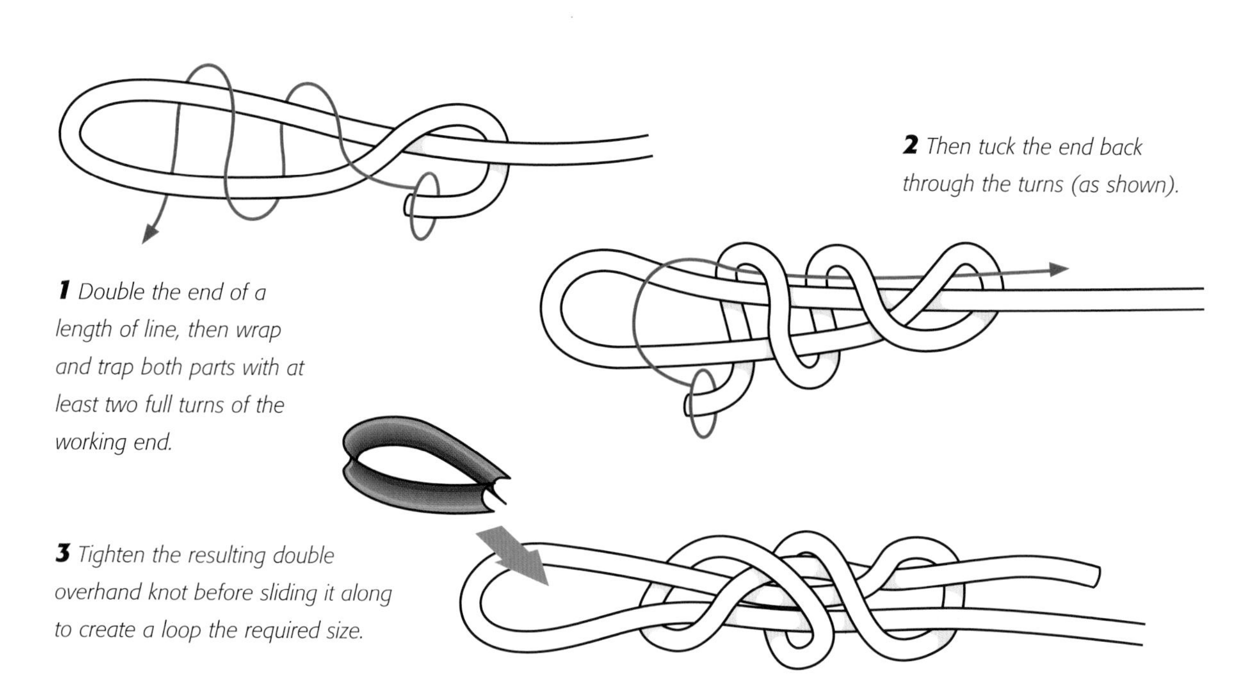

2 Then tuck the end back through the turns (as shown).

1 Double the end of a length of line, then wrap and trap both parts with at least two full turns of the working end.

3 Tighten the resulting double overhand knot before sliding it along to create a loop the required size.

Expert tip

Boating enthusiasts are becoming aware that this knot is preferable to an eye splice which (in three-strand rope) inevitably stretches and loses its grip on a thimble, while the long taper of a braided rope eye splice often jams in the sheaves of blocks. A scaffold knot, on the other hand, tightens under load and consequently remains a snug fit forever, and its short length enables halyards to be hauled chock a block.

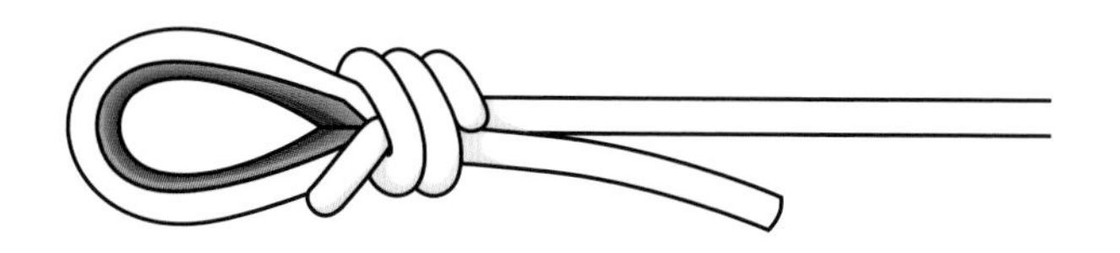

4 Insert a thimble, if needed, and ensure that the pointed jaws fit snugly into the knot, as the loop is tightened.

Carrick bend

This bend joins large and less flexible ropes and cables. It is also the basis for the knife lanyard knot and Turk's head (both described later in this section).

Expert tip
Make sure that the short ends emerge on opposite sides of this knot, as there is a long-held belief that it is more secure that way.

__1__ Form an overhand loop in the end of one rope and lay the working end of the other rope on top of it.

__2__ Interweave this second working end in a locking tuck that goes under-over-under-over-under.

__3__ Pull on the standing parts of both ropes to capsize the flat layout into a distinctly different, but more stable and secure, configuration.

Knot lore
Aboard square-rigged sailing ships this bend was used to join cables that had to go around the barrel or body of a capstan.

Zeppelin bend

This bend – like most of them – is best when done in matching cordage ends, but it will tolerate some difference in diameter and construction. It is a heavy-duty knot, so use it with confidence to link mooring lines, towlines, and other working ropes, but it holds in small stuff too.

Expert tip
This bend can be loaded as soon as it is tied, before it is fully tightened, which – when things happen fast, as they sometimes do afloat – is a reassuring quality in a knot.

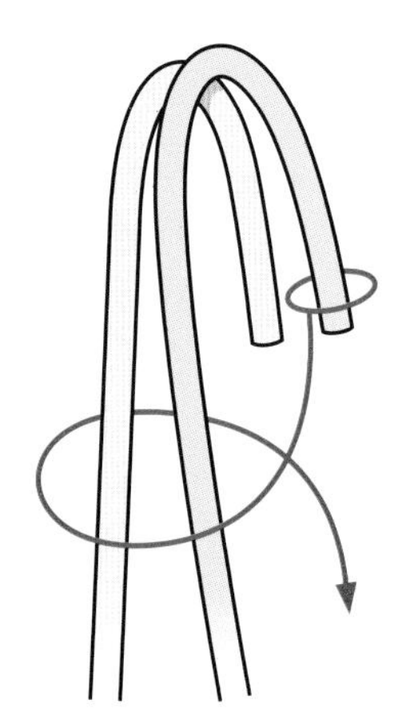

1 Grasp both ropes together, ends drooping in the same direction.

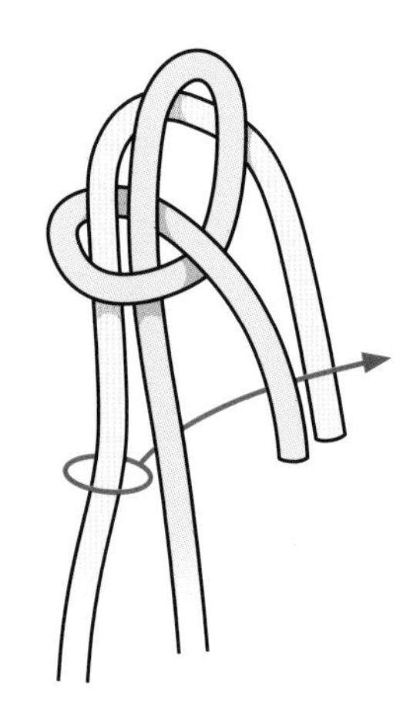

2 Tie a half-hitch in the nearer one, around both standing parts.

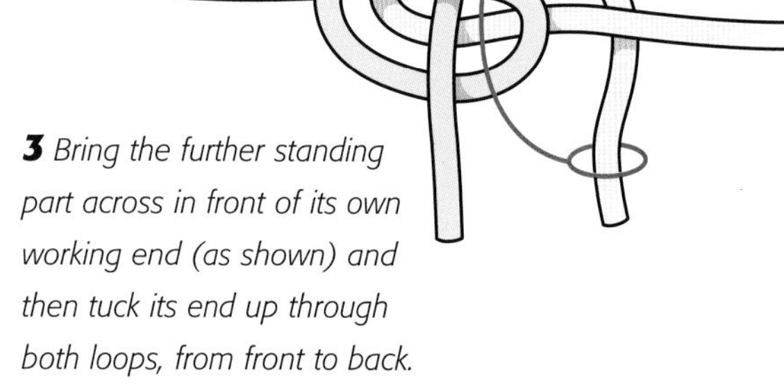

3 Bring the further standing part across in front of its own working end (as shown) and then tuck its end up through both loops, from front to back.

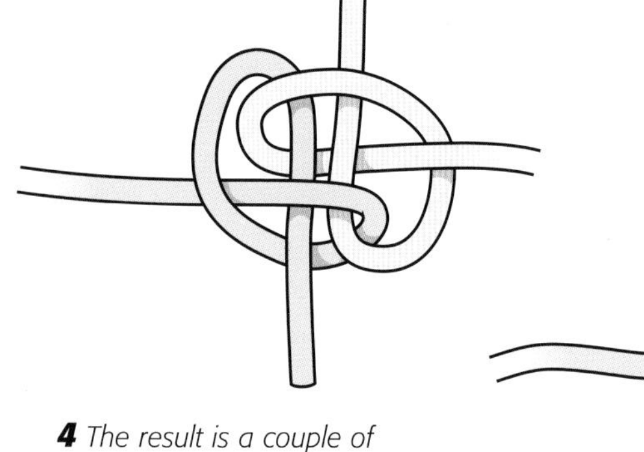

4 The result is a couple of interlocked overhand knots.

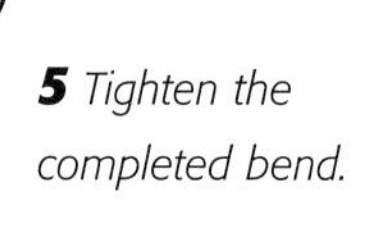

5 Tighten the completed bend.

Knot lore
The US Navy employed this knot in the 1930s to moor its lighter-than-airships, one of which was the gigantic dirigible *Los Angeles*, when it was known as the Rosendahl bend (after her master and commander). The imaginative title Zeppelin bend first appeared in a 1976 article about the knot by Lee and Bob Payne in *Boating* magazine.

Knife lanyard knot

This tough – but equally ornamental – alternative to the Chinese cross knot (*see page 42*) makes a loop to attach a clasp knife or other implement to a lanyard.

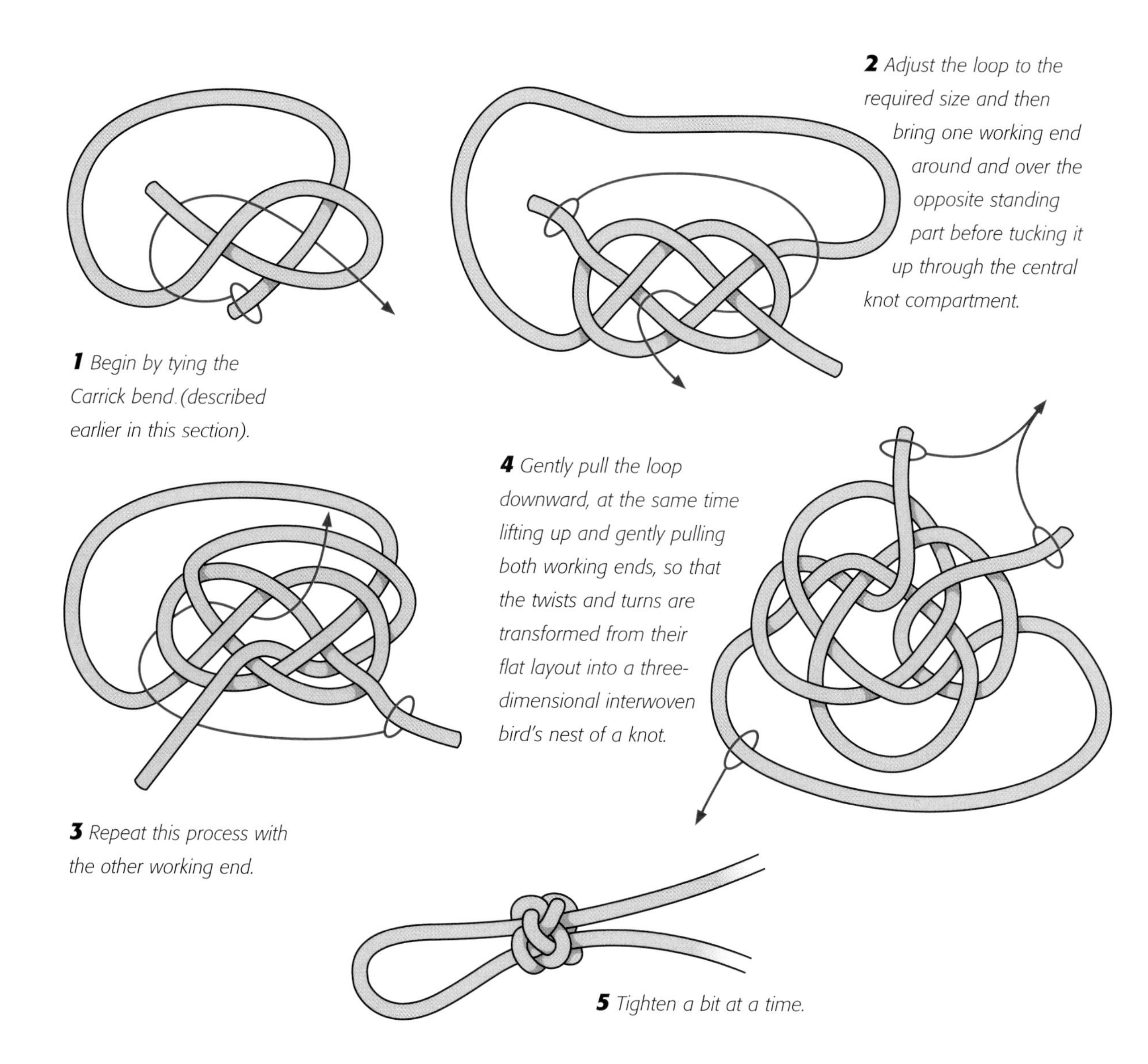

1 *Begin by tying the Carrick bend (described earlier in this section).*

2 *Adjust the loop to the required size and then bring one working end around and over the opposite standing part before tucking it up through the central knot compartment.*

3 *Repeat this process with the other working end.*

4 *Gently pull the loop downward, at the same time lifting up and gently pulling both working ends, so that the twists and turns are transformed from their flat layout into a three-dimensional interwoven bird's nest of a knot.*

5 *Tighten a bit at a time.*

Turk's head knot

(three leads x five bights)

Tied flat, this decorative knot makes a neat thump mat, to protect wooden decking from being dented and scarred by an errant tackle block. As a plaited bracelet, it can be applied to a tiller bar or the spoke amidships on a yacht's steering wheel. Tied around wrist or ankle, it makes a nautical fashion statement.

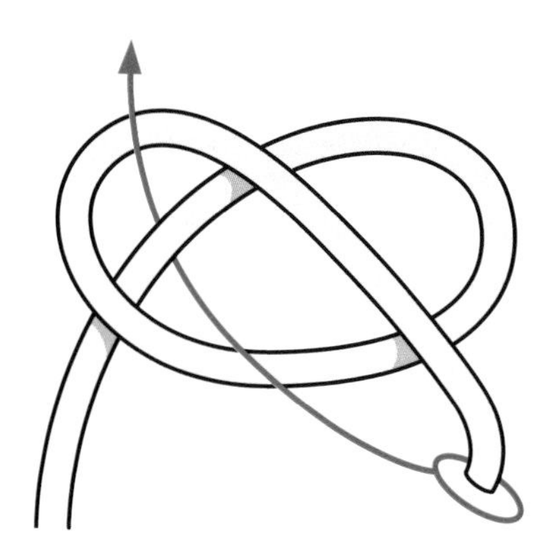

1 *Arrange a length of cord in the form of an uncompleted overhand knot.*

2 *Take one working end and tuck it, going over-under-over, then under-over-under-over, before tucking it alongside its own standing part.*

3 *With either end, follow around the original lead to render the knot two-ply or three-ply, and stitch, glue, or otherwise secure the two ends out of sight.*

Knot lore

As anyone east of Suez who wore a turban was labeled 'a Turk' by old-time sailormen, it seems that this simple Turk's head knot may have been named because of its resemblance to their headgear. There are countless more complicated Turk's heads and entire books have been written about this enormous family of knots.

LIFE-SUPPORT KNOTS

The older term for a selection of anchors and belays, hitches and holdfasts, such as those featured in this section, is 'climbing knots', but the label 'life-support knots' is superseding it as one that better represents the diverse practitioners of this kind of rope work: climbers and cavers; wilderness pioneers; extreme sports *aficionados*; civil engineers and scientists; coastguard or mountain rescue teams; and military assault squads. All of them may need to negotiate potentially hazardous terrain so as to gain access to out-of-the-way areas of work, study, and recreation.

Alpine coil

There are many ways to coil a climbing rope, and this is one neat and reliable technique that makes it easy to carry and keep tangle-free.

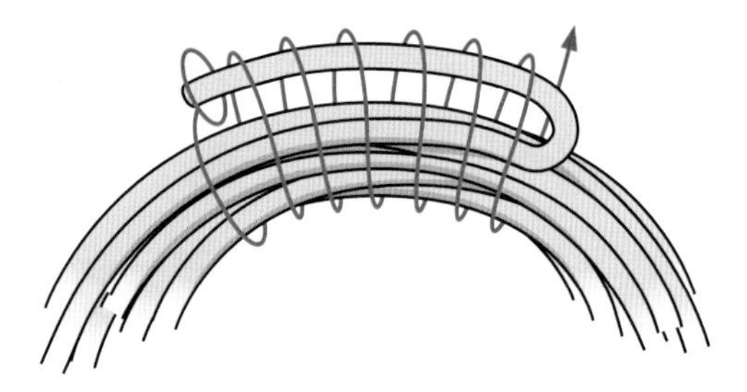

1 *Having first created a compliant series of turns, bend a long bight in the working end and locate it alongside the completed coil.*

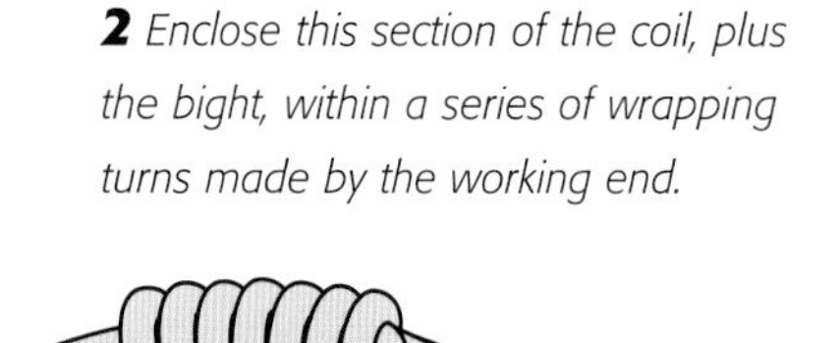

2 *Enclose this section of the coil, plus the bight, within a series of wrapping turns made by the working end.*

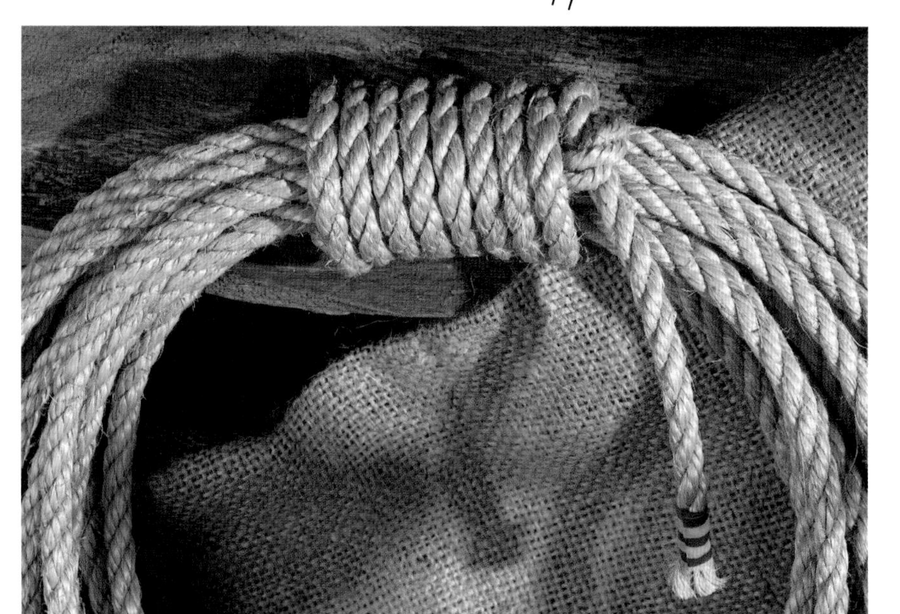

3 *Finally, tuck what remains of the end through the reduced bight and trap it there by pulling on the standing part of the bight.*

Expert tip

Rope, whether coiled or not, is best transported in a protective bag which will also keep it clean.

Ground line hitch

(on a coil)

Coiled rope should be hung up out of harm's way when not in use, and this technique for making a coil provides the necessary loop to do so.

1 Having made a coil, bend the working end back into a long bight, and then tie a half-hitch around the coil with the doubled rope.

2 Wrap and tuck this doubled part again, going over (and to the left of) the initial half-hitch, and then beneath itself. Tighten the resulting knot.

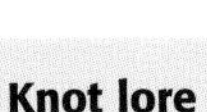

Knot lore

The ground line hitch, tied in a single cord around larger rope was used in the sea-fishing industry to secure trawl nets; and by horse soldiers and cowboys to tether their mounts to a picket line and so restrain them from straying.

Alpine butterfly loop

This classic climbing knot – tied in the bight, without using either end – forms a fixed loop for the middle member of a team (in glacier travel, for instance) to clip into with a carabiner. It will withstand a pull from any direction. The knot can also be used to bridge a damaged and weakened part of a rope.

Knot lore

In the USA this knot is also known as the 'lineman's loop (or rider),' signifying its use by telephone and telegraph repairmen.

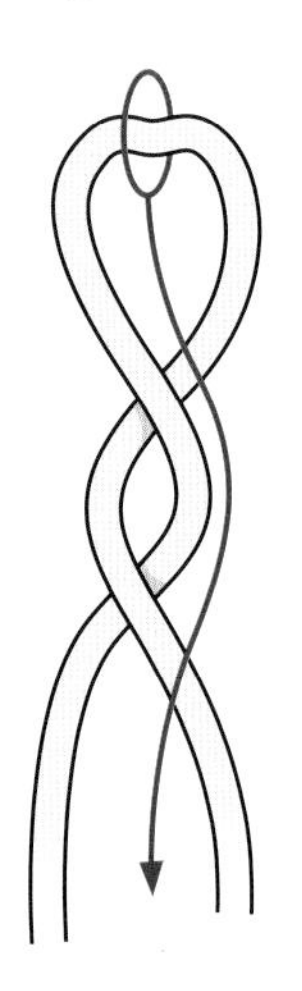

1 *Make a closed bight in the rope and impart a twist of 180°.*

2 *Invert the upper loop, bringing it down in front of the lower loop to lie on the two legs of the bight.*

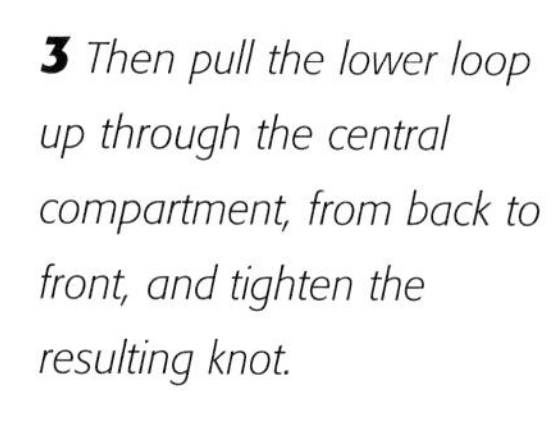

3 *Then pull the lower loop up through the central compartment, from back to front, and tighten the resulting knot.*

Expert tip

Anyone clipped into this knot can be inadvertently tugged to and fro by the movements of those ahead and behind. To obtain some slack, tie this knot with a longer loop, but keep the carabiners within a hand's reach. Use two carabiners with their gates reversed and opposed.

Overhand loop

This is the only satisfactory way to tie a loop in webbing to safeguard situations requiring anchorages or belays, as well as to improvise harnesses. It can also be tied in cordage.

Expert tip

When tying this knot in cordage, exclude superfluous twists before tightening by making the two twin rope parts swap sides when they come to a sharp bend (instead of continuing parallel like railroad lines).

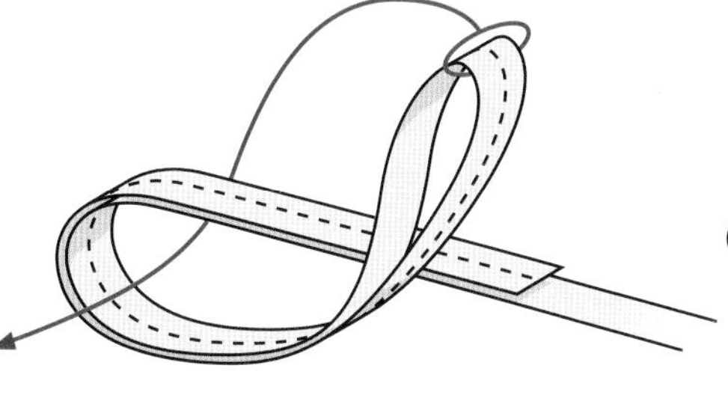

1 Bend a long bight in the end of the length of webbing, taking care to exclude needless twists.

2 Tie a simple overhand or thumb knot with the doubled length.

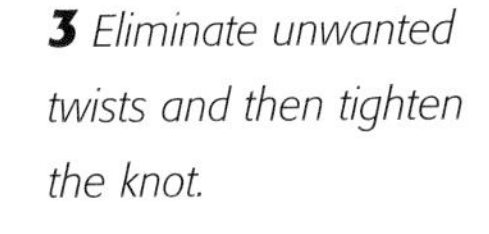

3 Eliminate unwanted twists and then tighten the knot.

Frost knot

This is how to assemble an endless sling, while at the same time incorporating a small fixed loop at one end, so as to improvise the portable stirrups known as étriers (short, looped climbing ladders). The knot can also be incorporated into knotted climbing harnesses.

Expert tip
Tug in turn each one of the six lengths of webbing that emerge from this knot to ensure that it draws up snug and tight. Carelessly tightened knots are weaker and less reliable than those that have been thoughtfully executed.

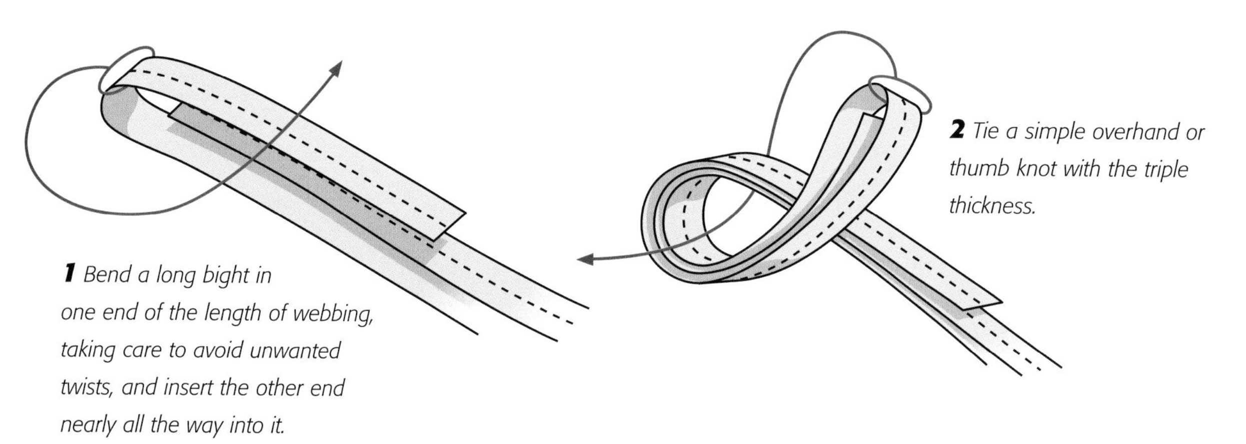

1 *Bend a long bight in one end of the length of webbing, taking care to avoid unwanted twists, and insert the other end nearly all the way into it.*

2 *Tie a simple overhand or thumb knot with the triple thickness.*

3 *Tighten the knot.*

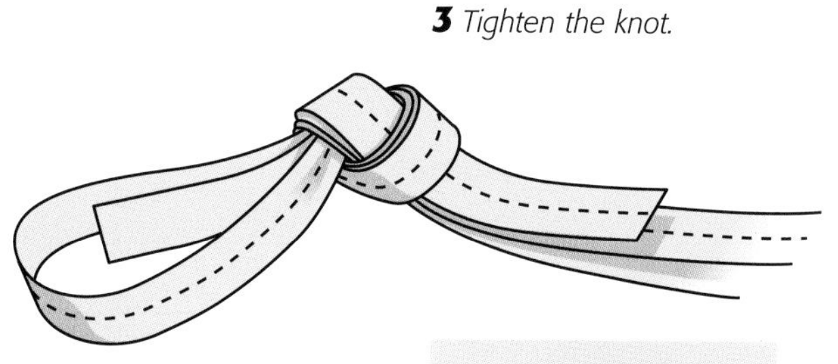

Knot lore
Climbers use numerous eponymous knots (knots named after people) and this one was dedicated to Tom Frost (some time in the 1960s).

Figure-eight loop

This knot is widely preferred for tying a fixed loop into the end of a rope, because it is easy to learn and then recall in the most challenging of circumstances. Its familiar form can also be readily checked by a leader or buddy. Fasten it to inanimate anchorages and secure belayed climbers with it.

Expert tip

Note how the doubled rope parts of this knot do not lie parallel like railroad lines, but swap sides each time they enter or leave a curve, rendering it snug and streamlined.

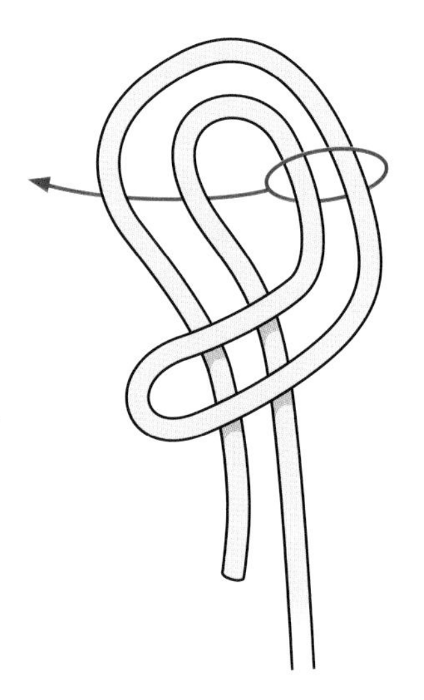

1 *Form a long bight in the end of the rope and impart half-a-twist.*

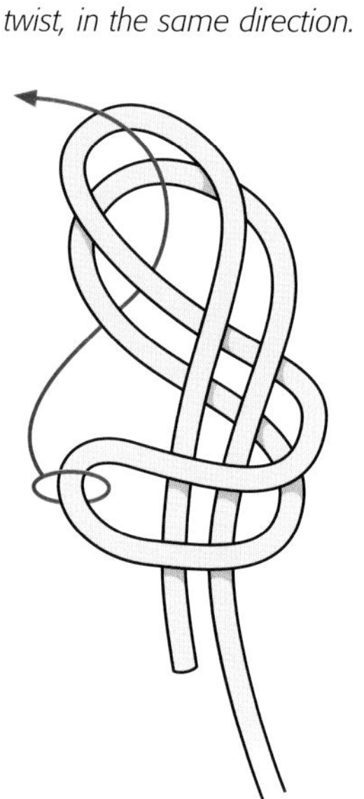

2 *Impart a second half-twist, in the same direction.*

3 *Tuck the end of the bight up through the initial loop.*

4 *Tighten the knot, taking care to eliminate needless twists, and leave the working end long enough to secure it to the standing part of the line with a double overhand knot.*

Knot lore

This knot is also referred to in print as the 'guide knot,' implying its use by professional climbers.

Double figure-eight loops

Twin fixed loops have several applications. They can be used to lift or lower an incapacitated member of the team, either as an improvised chair knot, with one loop around the chest and armpits, the other serving as a seat, or at either end of a suitable stretcher. They can also be employed to belay at a couple of anchorage points. And they may be employed to hoist and lower equipment.

Expert tip

Bear in mind that ill-dressed and inelegant knots may be less reliable than neat ones, so eliminate any unwanted twists from the numerous parts of this strong but somewhat bulky knot.

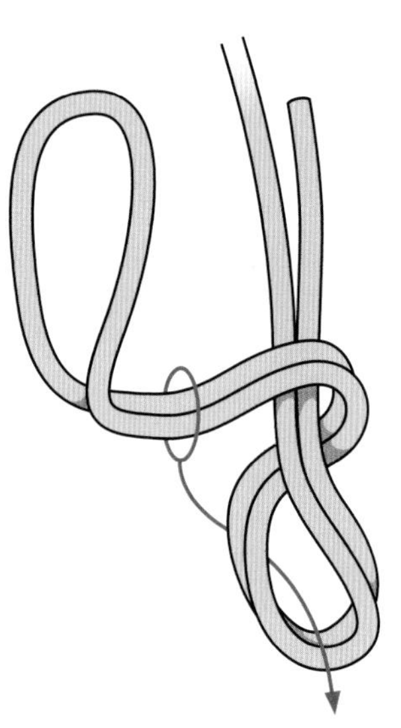

1 *Make a long bight in the end of the rope and impart a half-twist in the doubled length to create an underhand loop.*

2 *Continue, as if about to complete a simple figure-eight knot, but tuck a double draw-loop (instead of the bight's end) to form twin loops.*

3 *Bring the end of the initial bight down in front of the nearly complete knot, and lift both loops (from front to back) up through the bight.*

4 *Dress and tighten the knot.*

Triple bowline

Like the double figure-eight loops previously described, a triple bowline can be used to lift or lower an incapacitated member of the team, either as an improvised chair knot, with one loop around the chest and armpits, the other two serving as a seat, or suspending a suitable stretcher. It can also be used to belay to a trio of anchorage points, and may be used for hoisting and lowering equipment.

Expert tip

It is usual to tie all three loops of this knot more or less the same size because that is easiest. The third loop can, of course, be a lot longer or a little shorter than the other pair; but to arrange it so that all three are dissimilar would need to be done with some forethought early in the tying process, since it would be too fiddly to be worth the trouble of doing it once the knot had been tied and tightened.

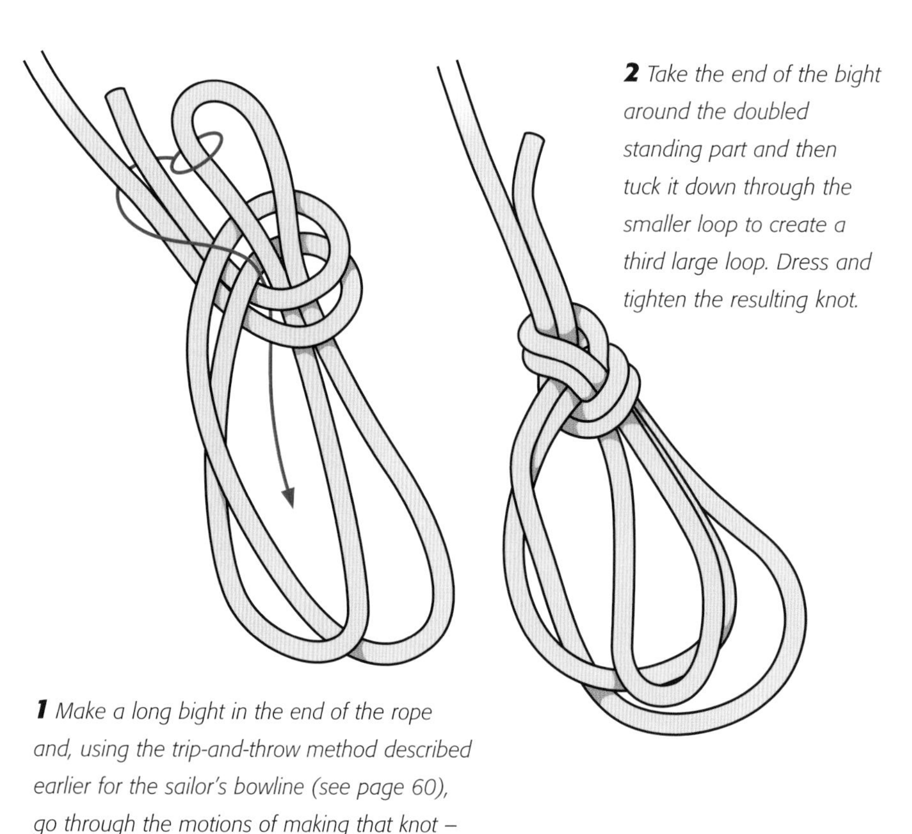

1 *Make a long bight in the end of the rope and, using the trip-and-throw method described earlier for the sailor's bowline (see page 60), go through the motions of making that knot – but with the doubled end or bight.*

2 *Take the end of the bight around the doubled standing part and then tuck it down through the smaller loop to create a third large loop. Dress and tighten the resulting knot.*

Tape knot

This is the only bend recommended by climbing councils and clubs to join two lengths of webbing (although it works well in cordage too), and it is an alternative to the figure-eight bend described later in this section. Also use it to make an endless sling.

Expert tip
Eliminate any unwanted twists before tightening this bend.

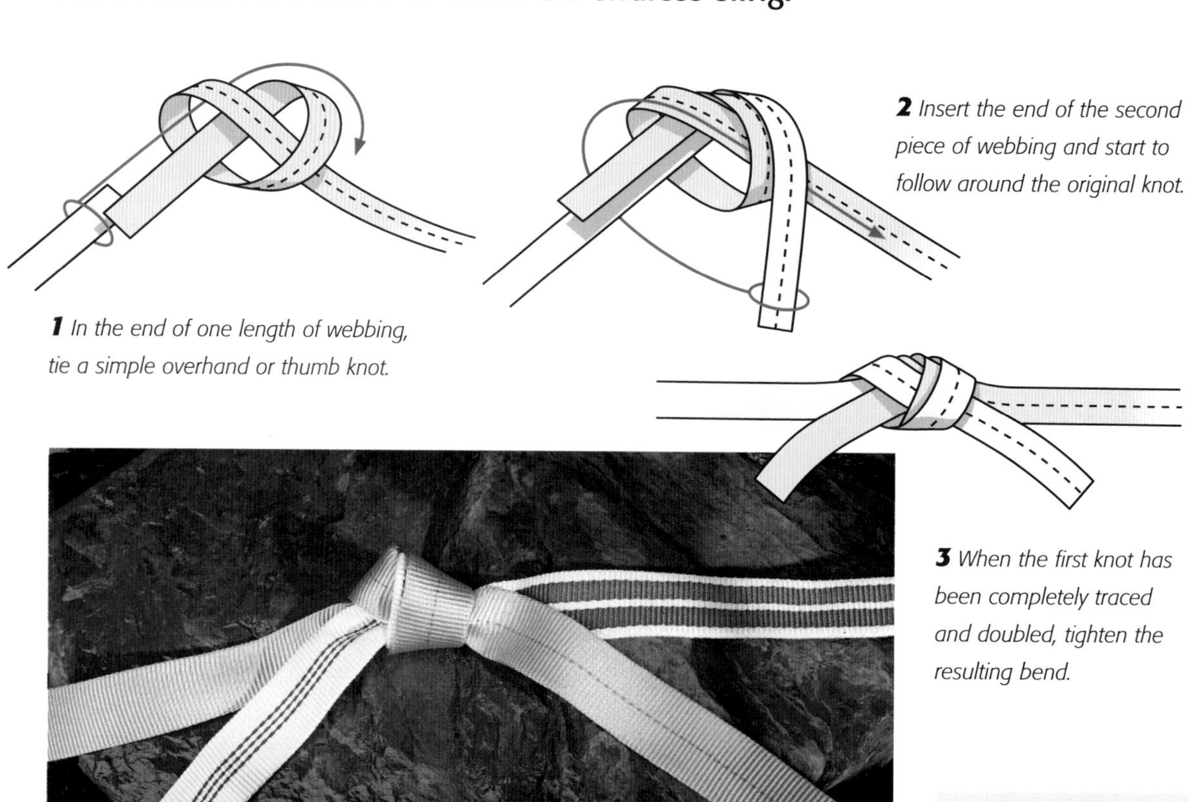

1 In the end of one length of webbing, tie a simple overhand or thumb knot.

2 Insert the end of the second piece of webbing and start to follow around the original knot.

3 When the first knot has been completely traced and doubled, tighten the resulting bend.

Knot lore
This knot is also known as the 'ring bend' or 'overhand bend' and (by anglers) as the 'water knot.'

Overhand shortening

This knot – in webbing – is the equivalent of a sheepshank in cordage. It will not only shorten flat stuff but at the same time provide two loops that can be used to clip into with carabiners if required. A damaged and weakened section of webbing may also be bridged, until it can be replaced, by means of this useful knot.

Knot lore
This knot has also been referred to in print as the 'double Frost knot.'

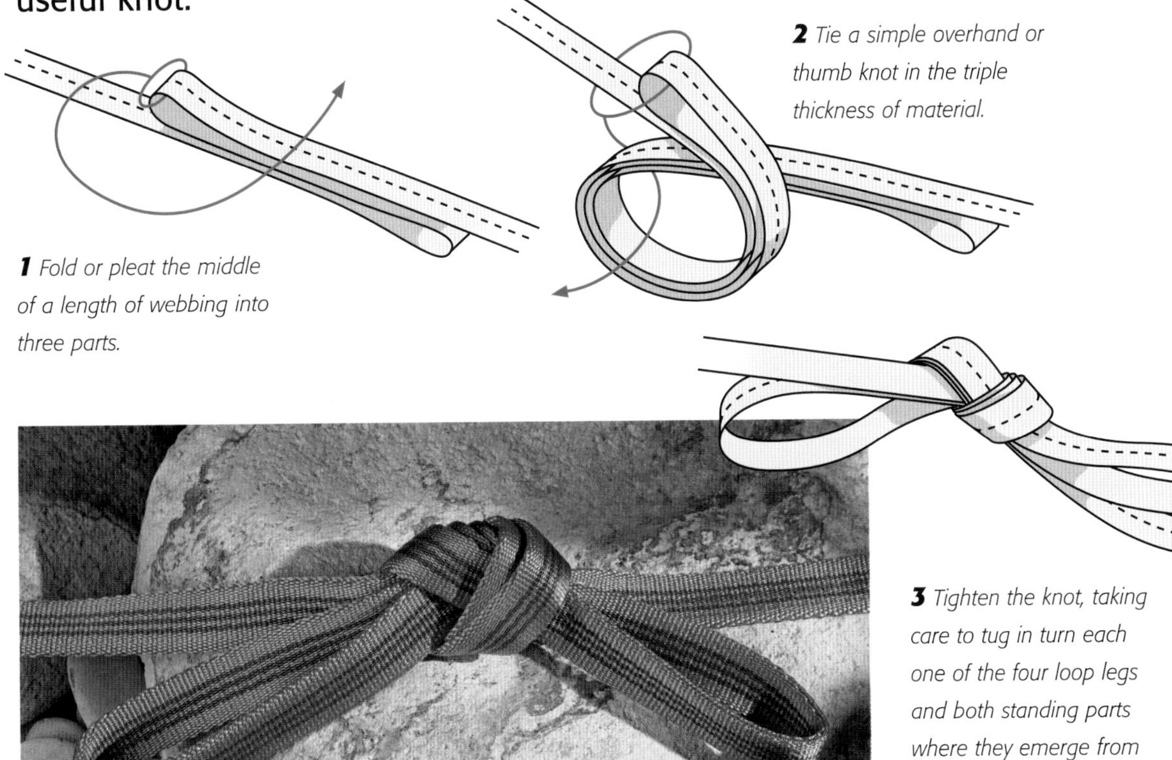

1 *Fold or pleat the middle of a length of webbing into three parts.*

2 *Tie a simple overhand or thumb knot in the triple thickness of material.*

3 *Tighten the knot, taking care to tug in turn each one of the four loop legs and both standing parts where they emerge from the knot.*

Reever bend

Join two ropes together with this strong and secure bend. They should be of similar diameter and construction, although a reever bend will work tolerably well in a couple of somewhat dissimilar ropes or cords.

Knot lore

The knot was introduced to climbers by Messrs C.E.I. Wright and J.E. Magowan in issue 40 of the *Alpine Journal,* dated May 1928, when it was apparently a new discovery intended for use in the three-strand flax ropes of that period.

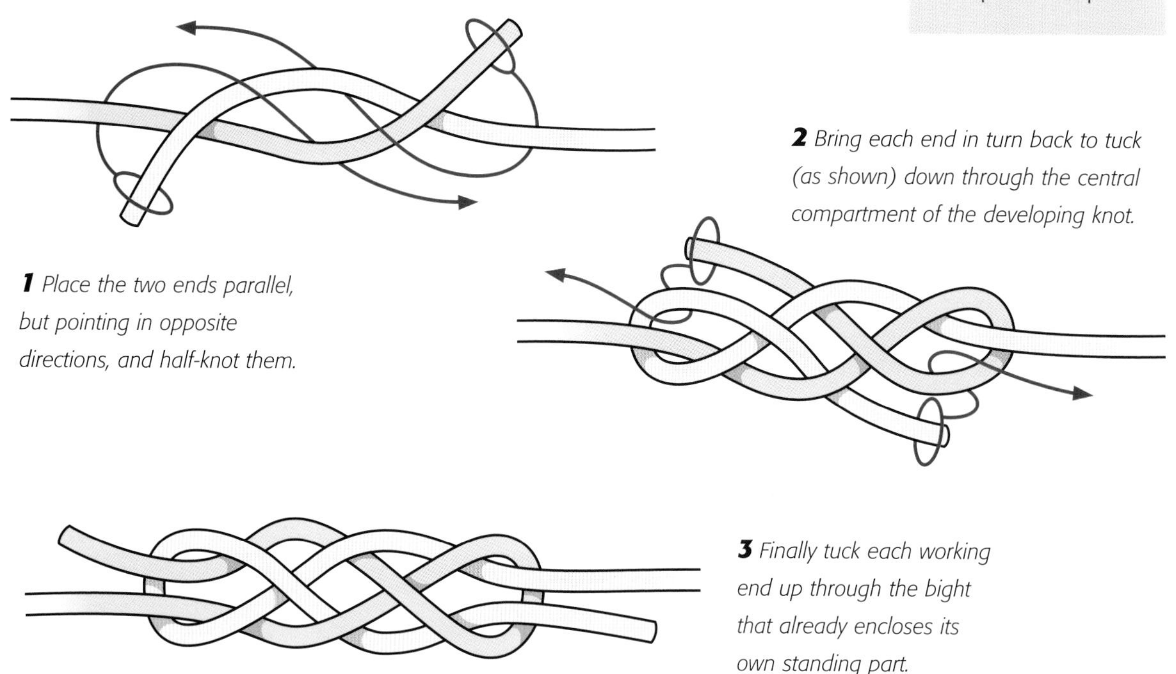

1 *Place the two ends parallel, but pointing in opposite directions, and half-knot them.*

2 *Bring each end in turn back to tuck (as shown) down through the central compartment of the developing knot.*

3 *Finally tuck each working end up through the bight that already encloses its own standing part.*

Expert tip

The reever bend has an elegant symmetry and is easy to tie but, although it has been around for at least 80 years, this knot is little known or used. It would be worthwhile to resurrect it and then evaluate in controlled conditions its fitness for today's synthetic sheath-and-core or braid-on-braid climbing ropes and cords.

4 *Tighten the knot.*

Figure-eight bend

(reinforced)

This is an established alternative to both the tape knot and the reever bend already described.

Knot lore

Sailors once knew this knot as the Flemish bend and do not seem to have liked it much, perhaps deeming it too bulky and bothersome to tie for seagoing usage.

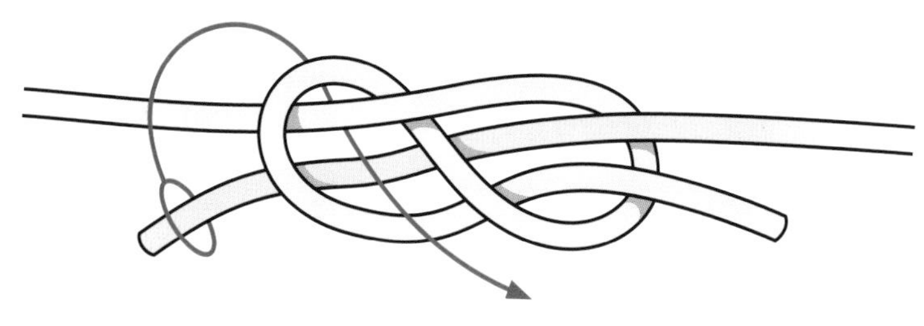

1 *Bring the two ends together, parallel and facing in opposite directions, and tie a figure-eight knot in one so that it encloses the other.*

2 *With the other end, follow around and duplicate the knot already tied.*

3 *Dress and tighten the resulting knot.*

Expert tip

Eliminate unwanted twists, but ensure that duplicate knot parts swap sides in the sharp curves of the knot. Leave both ends long enough to be either taped or tied (with a pair of double overhand knots) to their adjacent standing parts for belt-and-braces security.

Reef knot

(reinforced)

Expert tip
Beware – the naked reef knot (not reinforced) is notoriously weak, reducing the breaking strength of any rope or cord in which it is tied by 50 percent or more. It is merely a binding knot, fit only to tie around the necks of duffel bags and refuse sacks, or for parcels, bandages, and shoe-laces (in the form of a double reef bow).

As sails are rarely reefed by means of cord 'reef points' these days, the knot now described has not been located in the section on Boating Knots. Astonishingly (in view of the ***Expert tip*** comments), it is actually recommended in one or two climbing manuals for joining two or more abseil (or rappel) lines to one another.

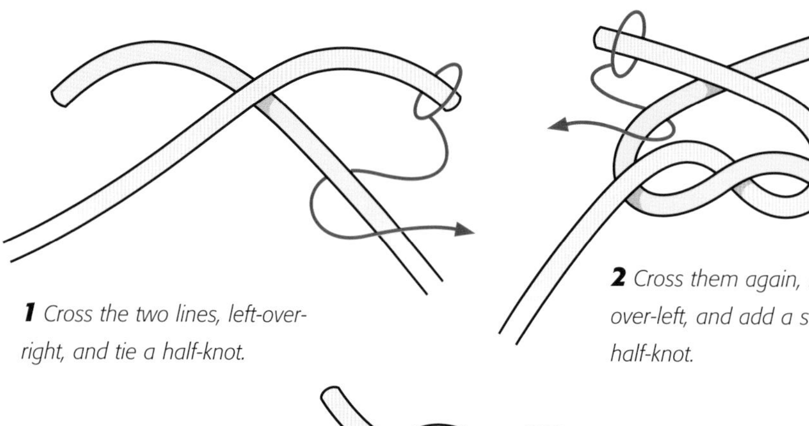

1 Cross the two lines, left-over-right, and tie a half-knot.

2 Cross them again, right-over-left, and add a second half-knot.

3 The resulting flat knot, consisting of two interlocked bights, is termed an SZ knot (because of the lay or handedness of each half-knot, in the order they were tied).

4 The mirror-image reef knot is a ZS version.

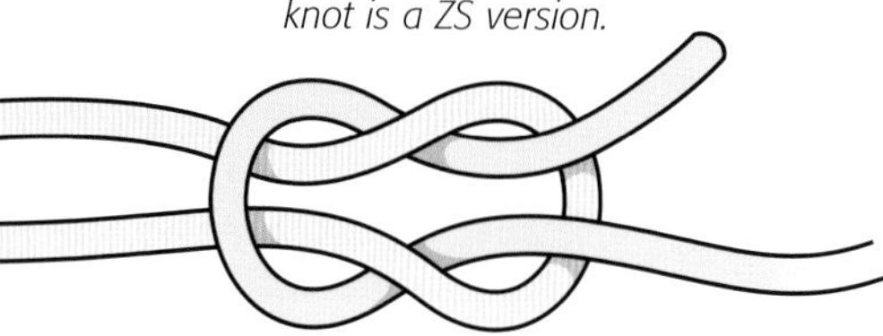

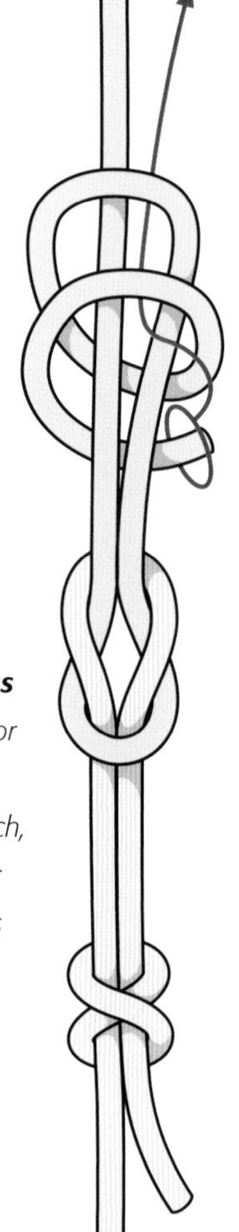

***5 Never use a reef knot as a bend** without backing up or locking off both ends. Leave the ends long enough to stitch, tape, or tie them (with a pair of double overhand knots, as illustrated) to their adjacent standing parts.*

Munter friction hitch

This dynamic contrivance will check and hold a load (live or inert) through friction. Using it the operator can feed out, or brake in a controlled fashion, a rope under tension – maybe even check a falling climber. It is bi-directional and, provided the carabiner is large enough, the hitch will flip over to facilitate pulling in unwanted slack.

Knot lore

This eponymous climbing knot was first introduced in 1974 at a meeting of the *Union Internationale des Associations d'Alpinisme* in Italy, which is why its other name is the Italian hitch.

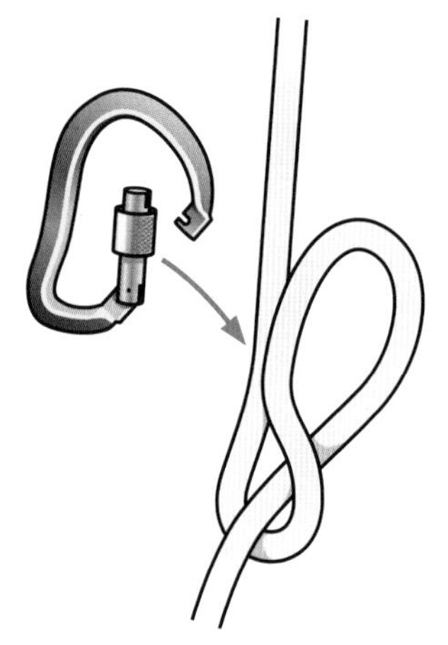

1 *Pull out a bight in the standing portion of the rope, twist it into an uncompleted figure-eight, then clip-and-lock a carabiner onto it (as shown).*

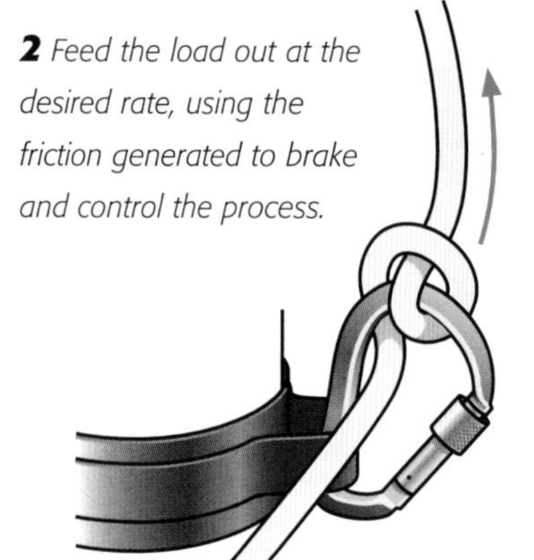

2 *Feed the load out at the desired rate, using the friction generated to brake and control the process.*

3 *To pull in slack, first cause the hitch to reverse its layout.*

4 *Hold firm and, whether pulling in or letting out, it will lock under load.*

Expert tip

There is some evidence that, subjected to a sudden severe load, this hitch may glaze or burn synthetic ropes. Some users doubt that and question how it could occur since the area of contact is constantly changing. Nevertheless, the sharp curves of this hitch do strain the geometry of climbing rope construction, and it would be prudent to discard any rope that had – while tied with it – been forced to absorb an extreme shock and thus been tested to the limit of its theoretical breaking strength.

Munter mule

If, while belaying or abseiling (rappelling) with a Munter friction hitch, it becomes necessary to free both hands for some vital task – resort to the Munter mule.

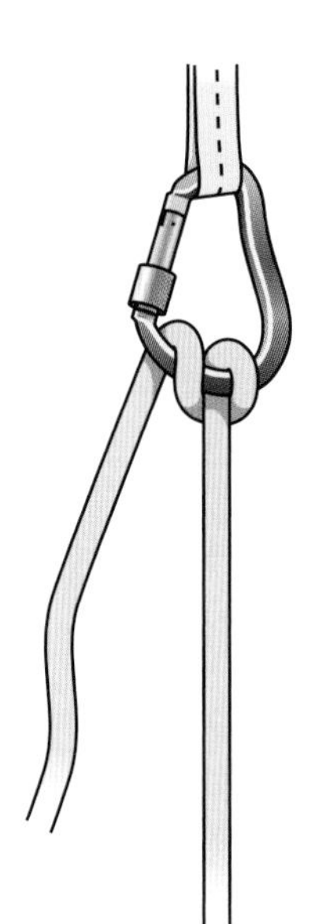

1 *Check (that is, brake) the operation of the hitch.*

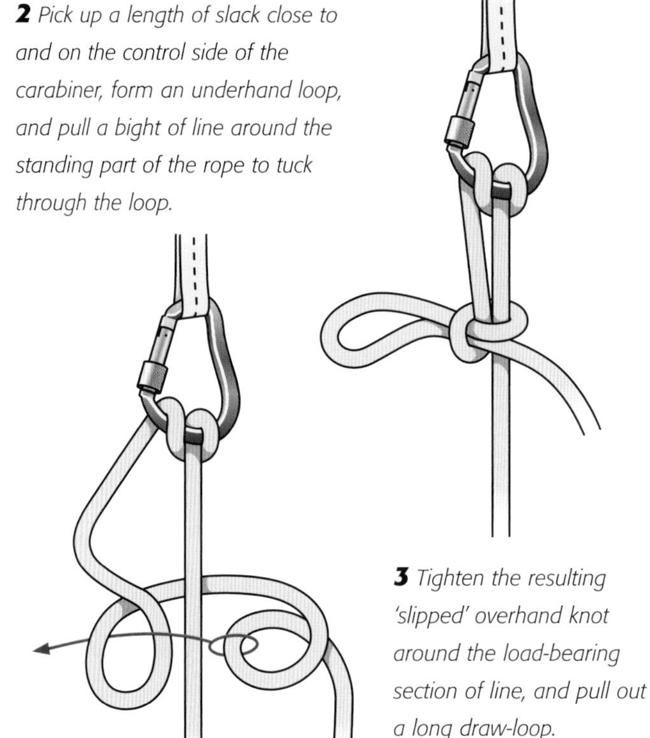

2 *Pick up a length of slack close to and on the control side of the carabiner, form an underhand loop, and pull a bight of line around the standing part of the rope to tuck through the loop.*

3 *Tighten the resulting 'slipped' overhand knot around the load-bearing section of line, and pull out a long draw-loop.*

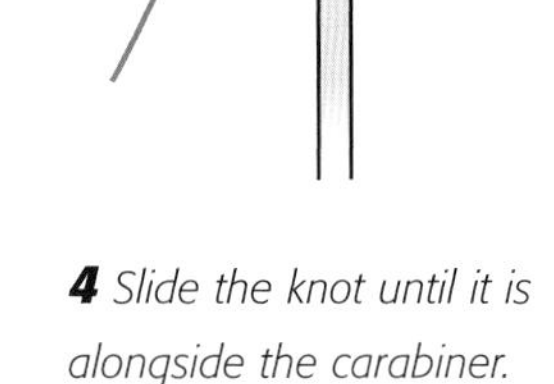

4 *Slide the knot until it is alongside the carabiner.*

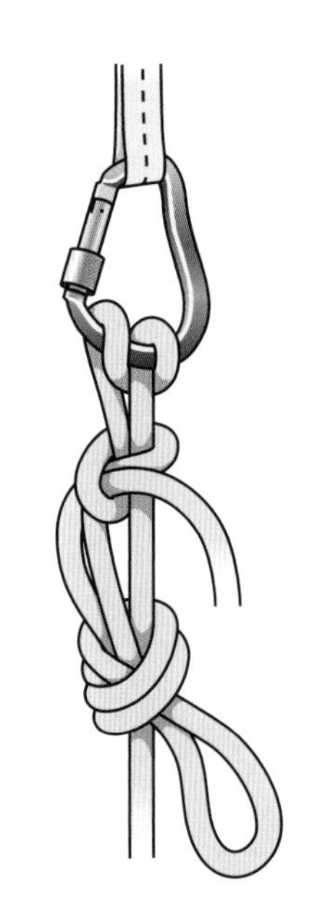

5 *Lastly, tie the draw-loop in a second overhand knot around the loaded line.*

Knot lore

The Munter friction hitch is one of several so-called 'knotless knots,' a contradictory yet catchy term for a category of knots – tied in the bight – that rely upon the insertion of an item of hardware (in this instance a carabiner) to retain their form. Without it, they fall apart, leaving only memories of themselves. The pile, post, or stake hitch (see page 58) is another such knotless knot.

CLIPPER WALES

FISHING KNOTS

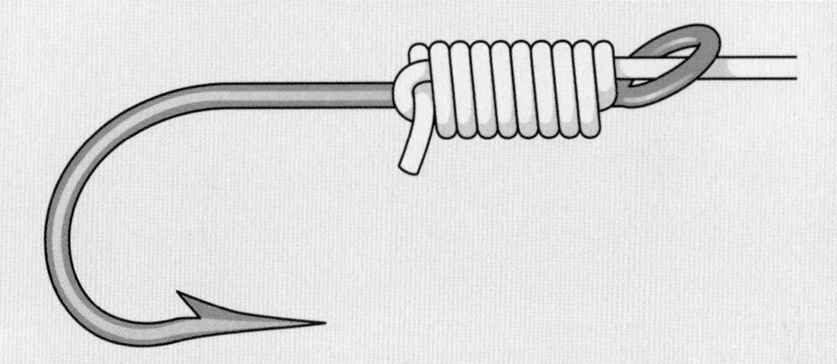

Most fishing knots are tied in fine nylon monofilaments and, despite a range of diameters for different breaking strengths, the knots are consequently tiny compared with those tied for other purposes in ordinary cordage. They are illustrated in this section using much thicker materials and, indeed, they are best learned in such stuff before attempting them in fishing line itself.

Tying fishing knots is a fiddly business and some of the deft, almost sleight-of-hand, movements acquired in time by anglers with tuition from fishing colleagues cannot be depicted on the pages of a book like this.

There is, however, one indispensable technique that can be explained – 'flyping' (rhyme it with 'typing'). Several seemingly disparate knots – from the improved clinch to the offshore swivel – use the same trick: two knot parts are twisted together but then, as the knot is pulled tight, one of the strands untwists to wrap around and over itself. To 'flype' means to turn a nascent knot inside out, a bit like peeling off a sock or glove.

Surgeon's loop

Knot lore
The verb 'flyping' first appeared in print over 100 years ago when it was used by the Scottish physicist Peter Guthrie Tait (1831-1901). It was resurrected by knot tyers in the mid-1980s to describe a knotting maneuver that otherwise cannot be simply explained in a few words.

This is a quick and easy way to tie a very strong and streamlined fixed loop in the end of a line to start a tackle system.

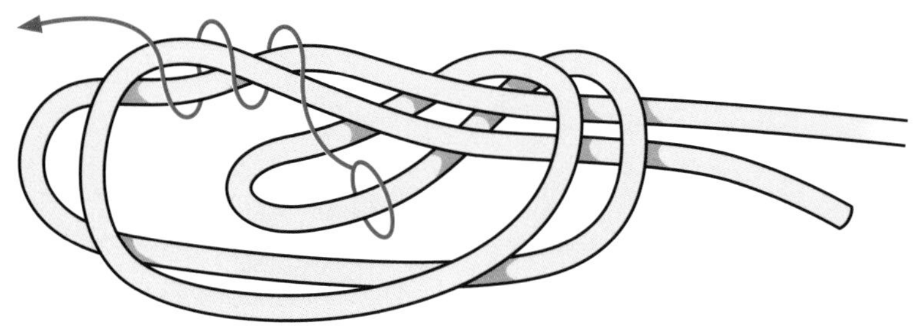

1 *Make a long bight in the end of the line and tie a simple overhand or thumb knot in the doubled length.*

2 *Tuck twice more to complete a triple overhand knot.*

3 *Pull both ends of the knot until it 'flypes' and begins to wrap around itself.*

4 *Dress and tighten the resulting knot.*

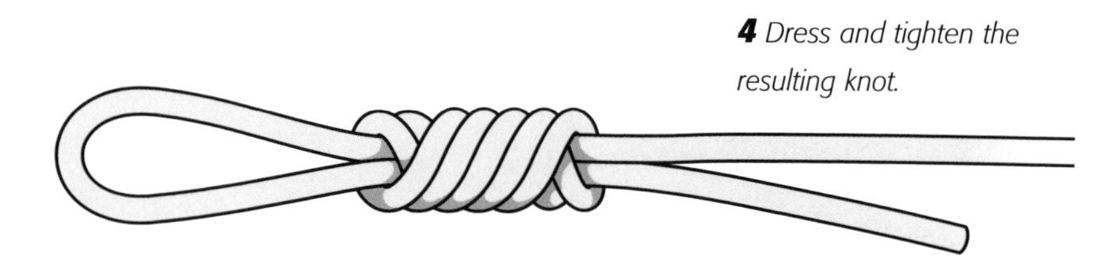

Blood loop dropper

This loop projects from the standing part of the line, for the attachment of extra flies, lures, baited hooks, and weights or sinkers.

Expert tip

This knot may also be tied with two separate ends, which must then be knotted together to create the required loop (*see the 'blood knot' described on page 120*).

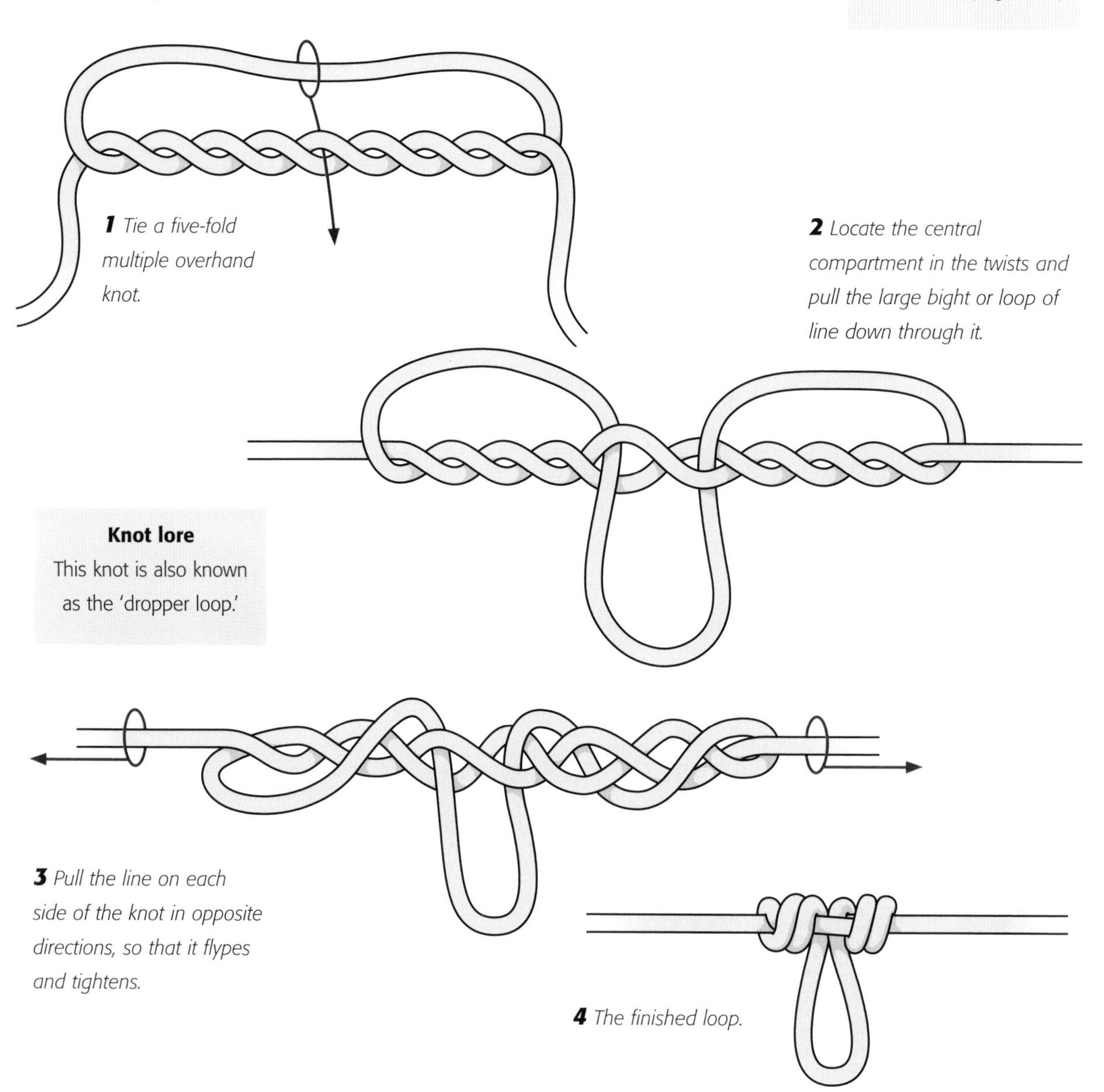

1 *Tie a five-fold multiple overhand knot.*

2 *Locate the central compartment in the twists and pull the large bight or loop of line down through it.*

Knot lore

This knot is also known as the 'dropper loop.'

3 *Pull the line on each side of the knot in opposite directions, so that it flypes and tightens.*

4 *The finished loop.*

Improved basic snell

The snell attaches a line to the shank of a hook in such a way that both are accurately aligned when a pull is applied.

Knot lore
Snelling dates from the days when spade-ended hooks (those without eyes) were commonplace, but it works equally well with eyes turned up or down.

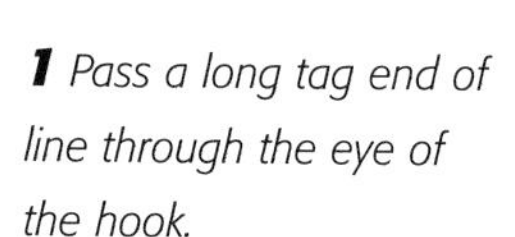

1 *Pass a long tag end of line through the eye of the hook.*

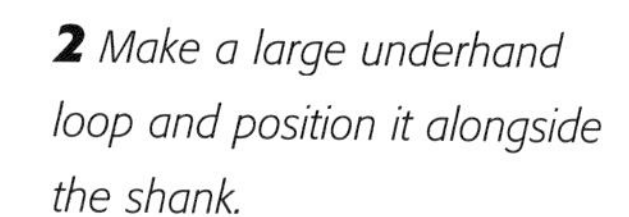

2 *Make a large underhand loop and position it alongside the shank.*

3 *With this loop, complete a series of snug wrapping turns to enclose hook shank, tag end, and the loop itself, passing each turn* cautiously and carefully *over the point of the hook (to avoid accidental injury).*

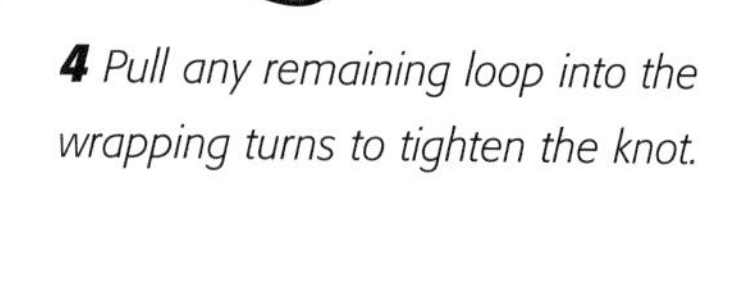

4 *Pull any remaining loop into the wrapping turns to tighten the knot.*

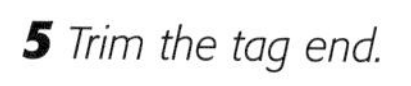

5 *Trim the tag end.*

Nail knot

The nail knot is a special application of 'snelling' (described on page 104). It is used to join a fly line to the butt section of the leader. Tie it with the aid of a nail or – better still – a short length of drinking straw, a small diameter metal tube, or the empty shell of a ballpoint pen.

Knot lore

The noted American fly fisherman Joe Brooks learned this knot in Argentina, where tying it was facilitated by means of a horseshoe nail – which is, presumably, how it acquired its original name. Nowadays it may also be referred to as the 'tube knot.'

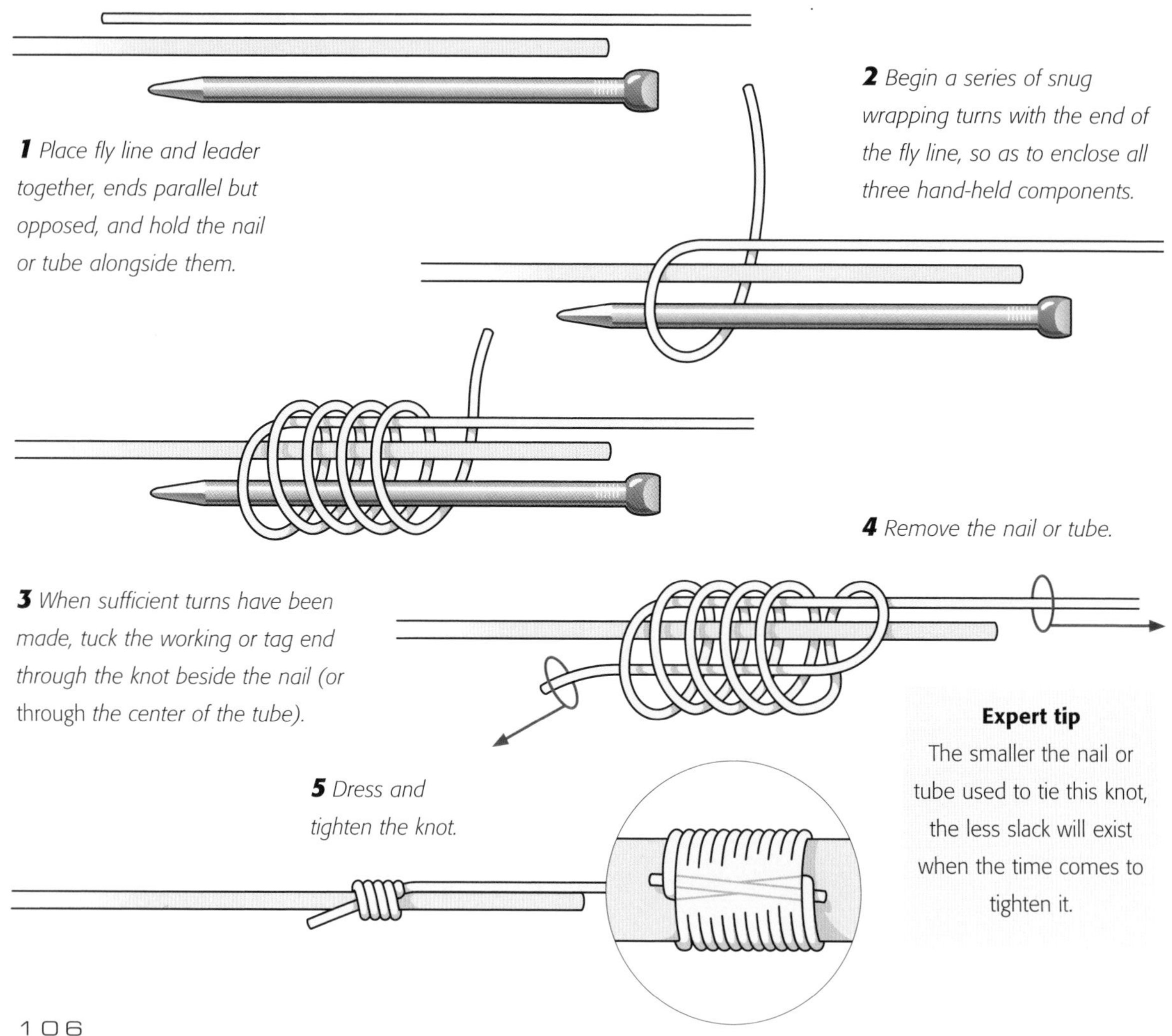

1 *Place fly line and leader together, ends parallel but opposed, and hold the nail or tube alongside them.*

2 *Begin a series of snug wrapping turns with the end of the fly line, so as to enclose all three hand-held components.*

3 *When sufficient turns have been made, tuck the working or tag end through the knot beside the nail (or through the center of the tube).*

4 *Remove the nail or tube.*

5 *Dress and tighten the knot.*

Expert tip

The smaller the nail or tube used to tie this knot, the less slack will exist when the time comes to tighten it.

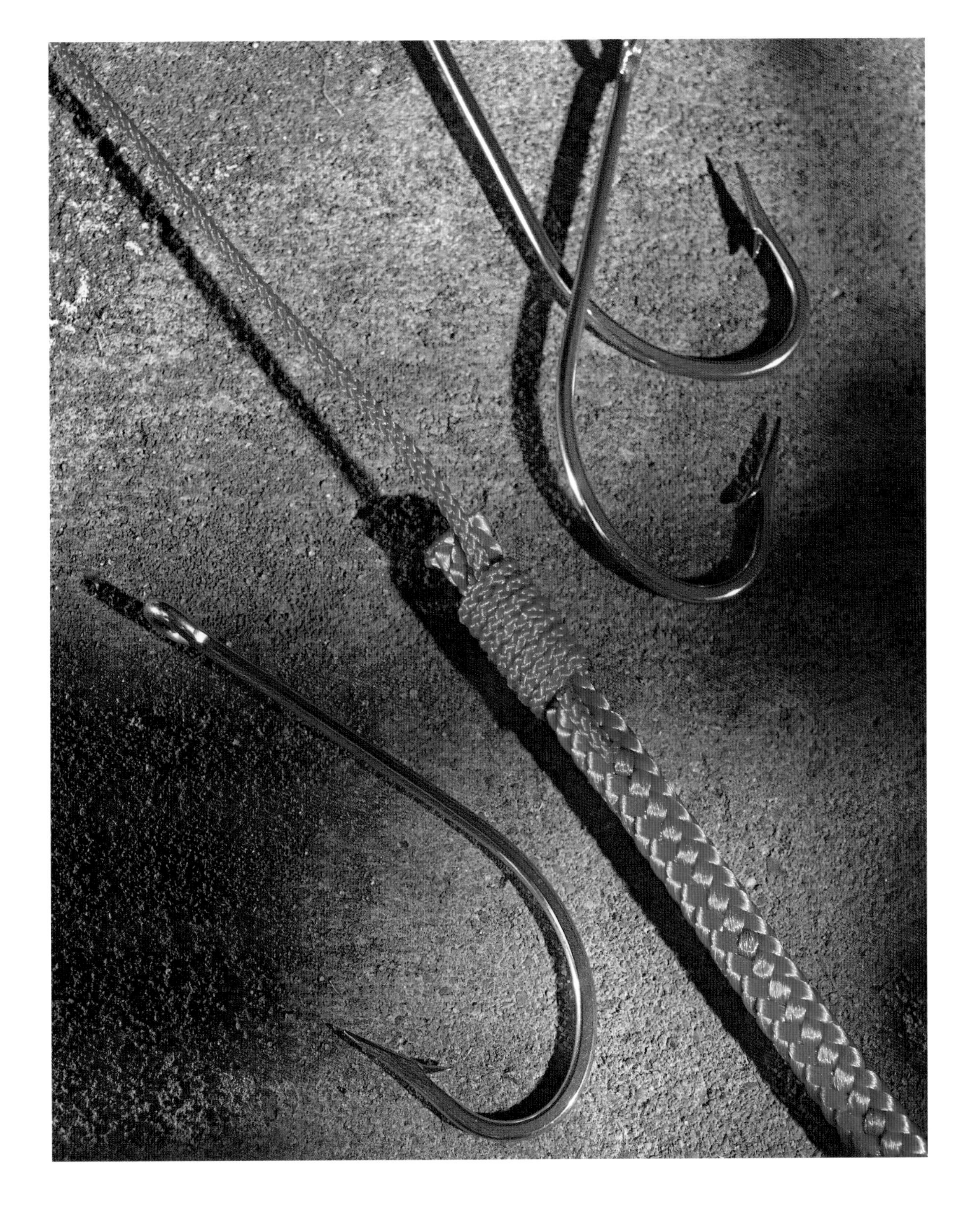

Domhof knot

Expert tip
Do not tuck the tag end through the eye of a flat-eyed hook, as this would make a straight-line pull impossible.

This knot, like the snell (*see page 104*), can be applied to either a spade-ended hook or one that has an eye (upturned or downturned).

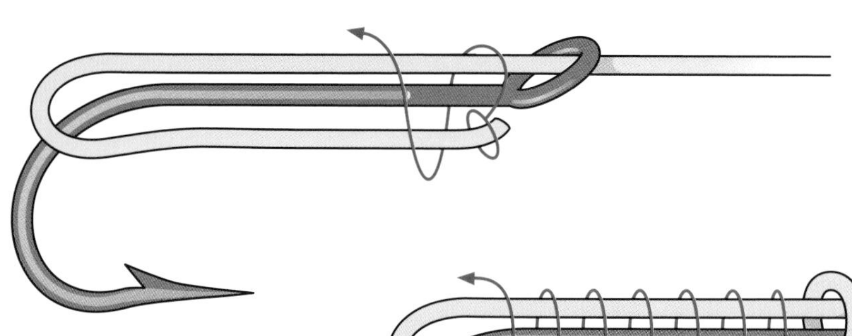

2 *With the end, make a snug series of wrapping turns, working from eye to hook (taking care not to become impaled upon it) and trapping both legs of the bight and the shank.*

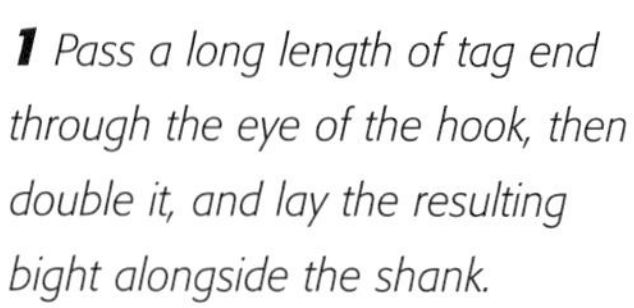

1 *Pass a long length of tag end through the eye of the hook, then double it, and lay the resulting bight alongside the shank.*

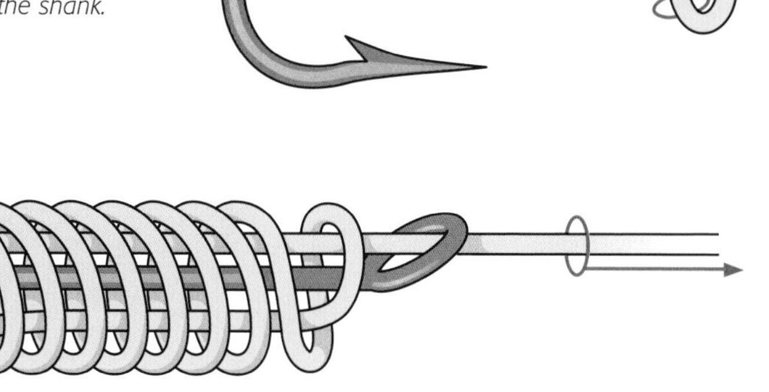

3 *Tuck the tag end through what remains of the bight and pull on the standing part of the line to tighten the knot.*

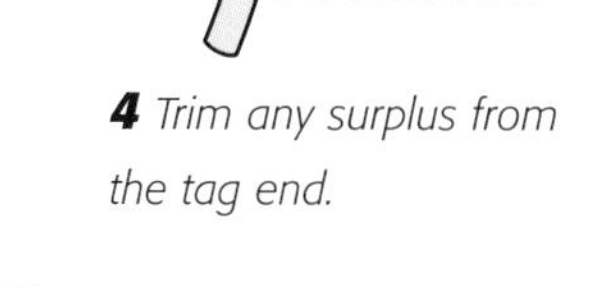

4 *Trim any surplus from the tag end.*

Non-slip mono knot

A small fixed loop like this one allows a hook, lure, or swivel to move freely and is preferable to some tighter knots. It is particularly helpful with lures which, their movement unrestricted, can move in a lifelike way.

Expert tip

To realize the breaking strength of almost 100 percent that is claimed for this knot, it is crucial to match the number of turns taken with the tag end around the standing part to the thickness of the line. Thin lines and braids accept six or seven turns, while medium ones require only four and the thickest lines need just two or three.

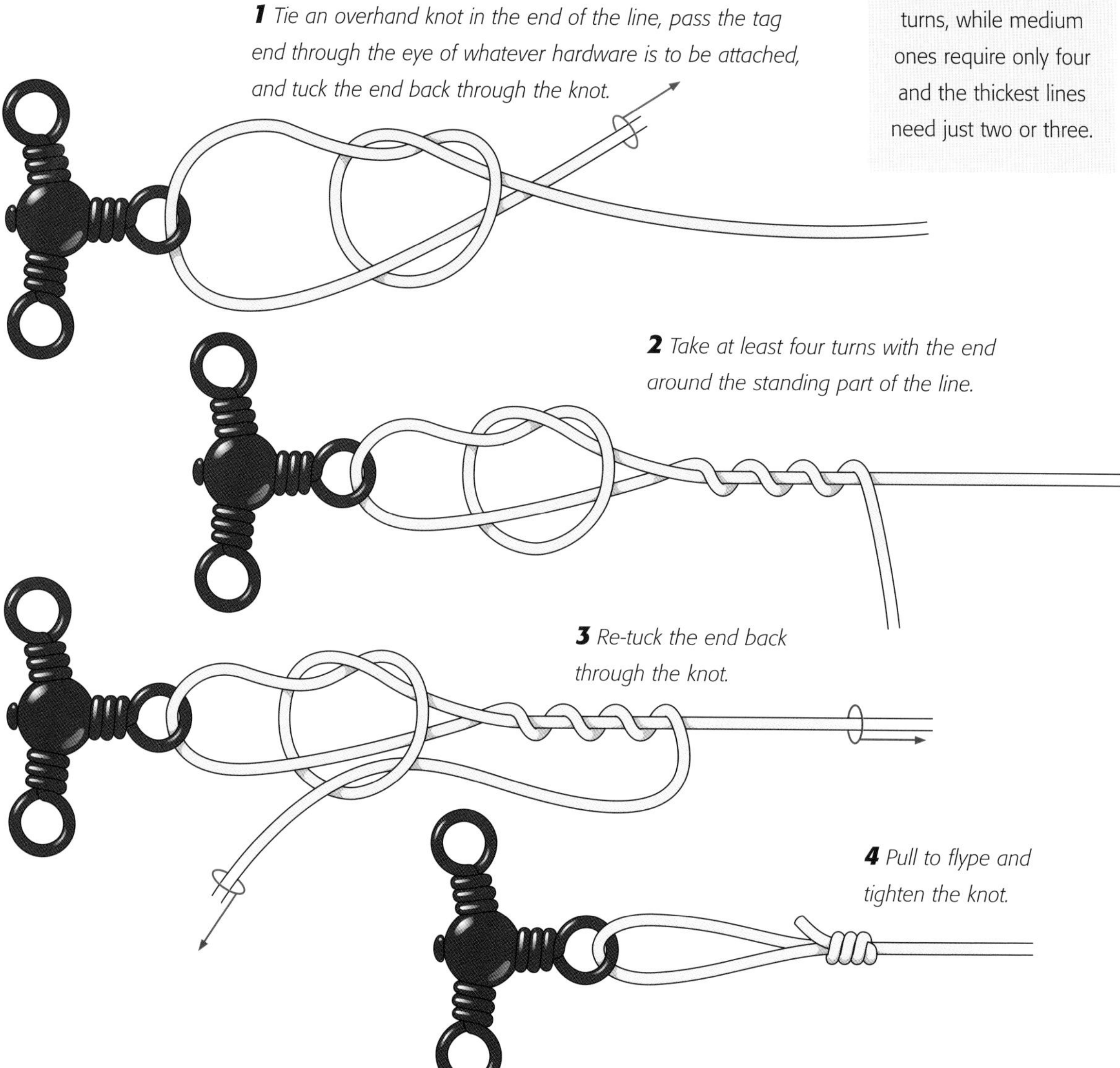

1 *Tie an overhand knot in the end of the line, pass the tag end through the eye of whatever hardware is to be attached, and tuck the end back through the knot.*

2 *Take at least four turns with the end around the standing part of the line.*

3 *Re-tuck the end back through the knot.*

4 *Pull to flype and tighten the knot.*

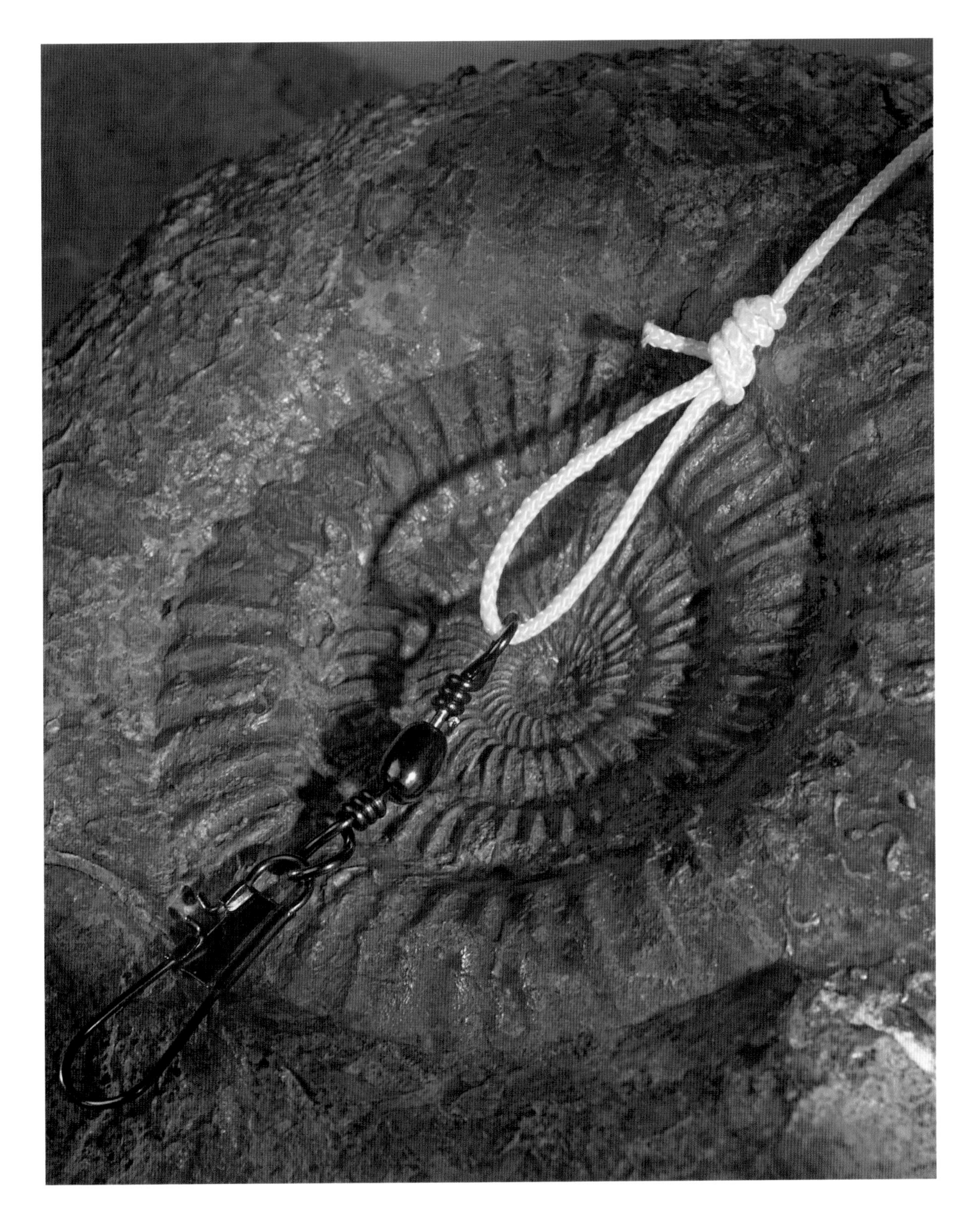

Improved clinch knot

This knot is used to attach a thinner line to a hook, lure, swivel, or other connector.

Expert tip
This is a strong knot but it can be hard to tighten in heavier lines.

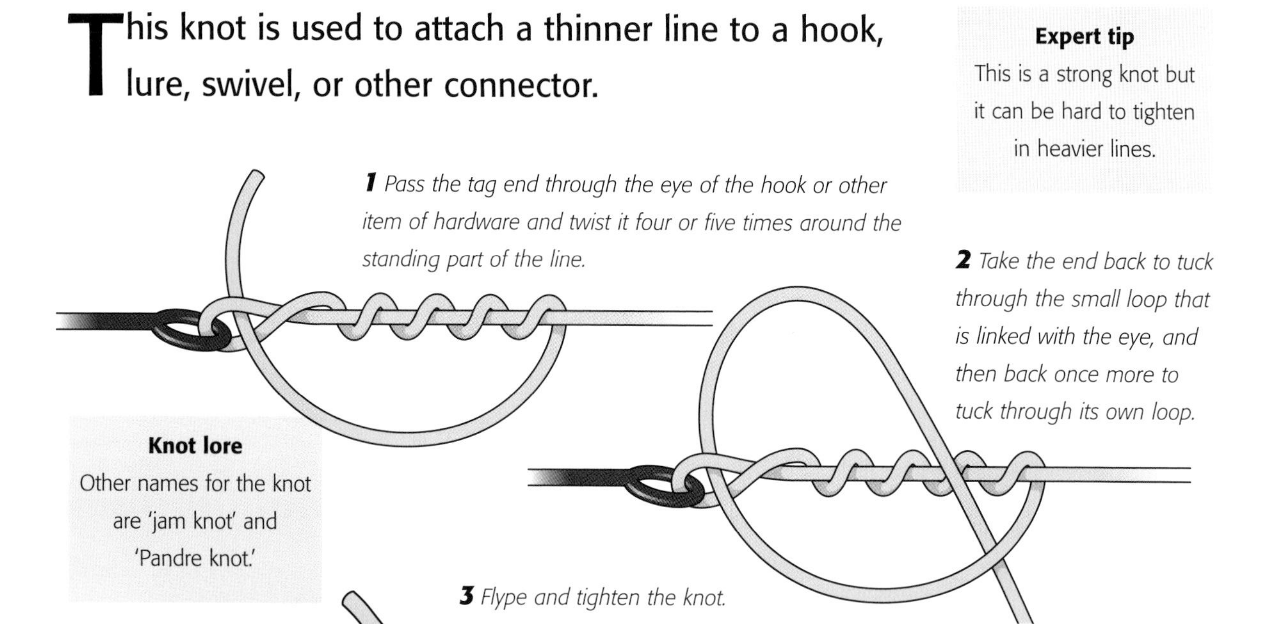

__1__ Pass the tag end through the eye of the hook or other item of hardware and twist it four or five times around the standing part of the line.

__2__ Take the end back to tuck through the small loop that is linked with the eye, and then back once more to tuck through its own loop.

__3__ Flype and tighten the knot.

Knot lore
Other names for the knot are 'jam knot' and 'Pandre knot.'

Hook, swivel, or braid knot

This strong and solid knot attaches monofilament line or braid to a hook, fly, or other lure.

Expert tip

Three or four wrap-and-trap turns can be sufficient in thick lines, while thinner ones may require eight or more.

1 *Make a long bight in the end of the line, pass this doubled thickness through the eye of the hook or ring, and lay it alongside its own standing part.*

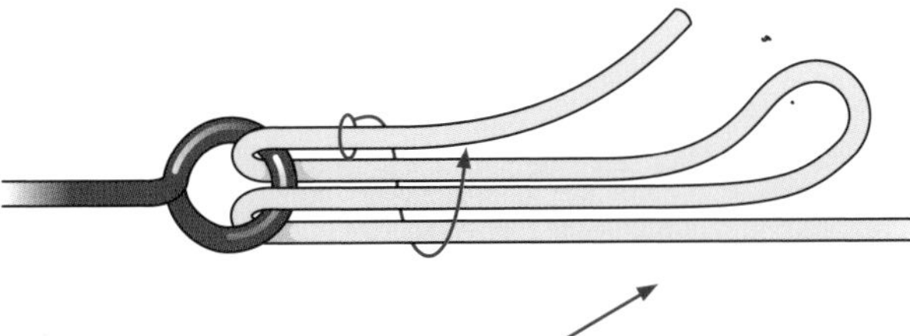

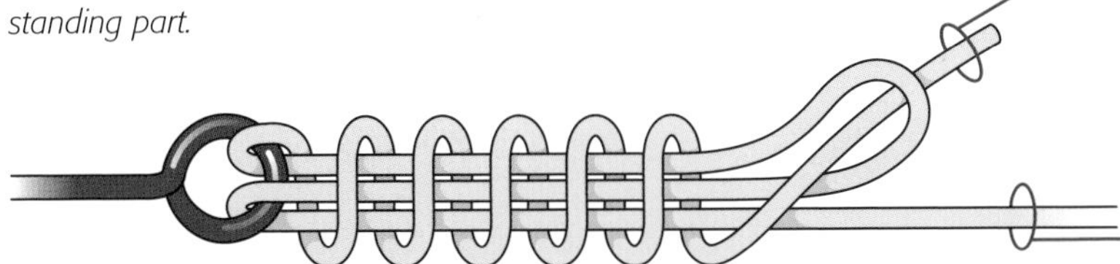

2 *With the tag end wrap a series of tucks to enclose and trap the other three sections of line, before tucking it through what remains of the bight.*

3 *Tighten the knot.*

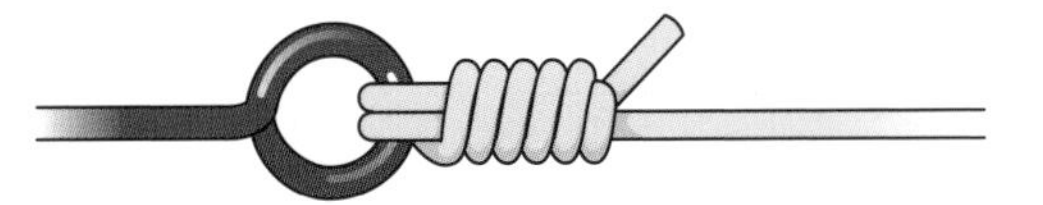

Offshore swivel knot

This ring hitch attaches the surgeon's loop (described on page 100) or any similar long loop knot to hooks and swivels for the tough conditions often experienced in big game fishing.

Expert tip
It is claimed for this knot that, should one loop or leg of the knot break, the other may hold, preventing the loss of tackle (and maybe a record-breaking catch).

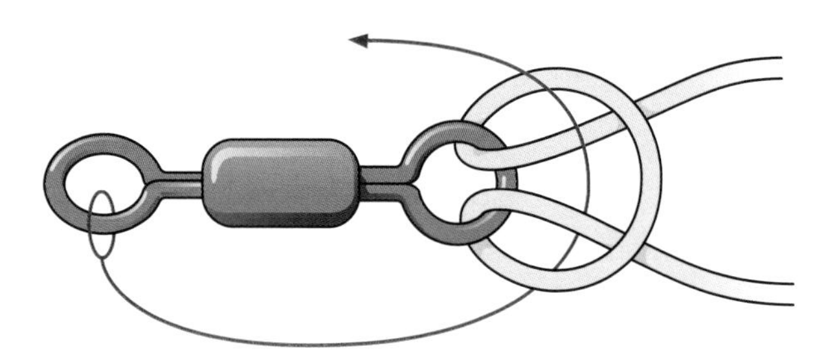

1 Pass the end of a long loop through the eye or ring and pull it down to lie on top of its own loop legs.

2 Rotate the hook, swivel, or other connector in a backward somersault up through the opening between the twin holding loops.

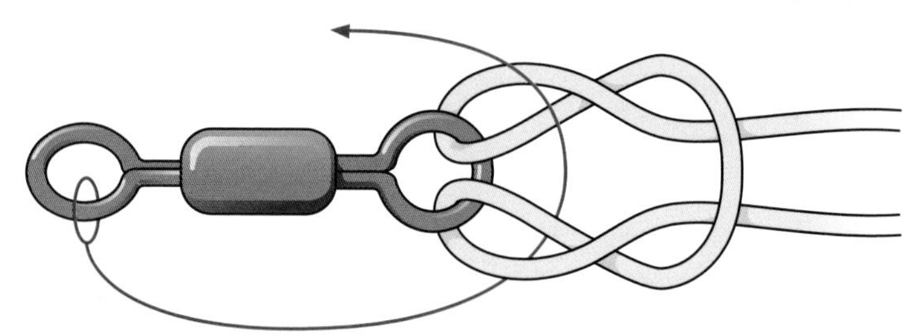

3 Repeat this turning and twisting process eight or so times.

4 Pull firmly on both long loop legs, straightening them, and shunt the resulting turns down to sit snugly against the hook or other item of hardware.

Knot lore
Anglers have their own knotty nomenclature, but tied in cordage – ashore or afloat – this knot has been known for centuries as a 'cat's paw.'

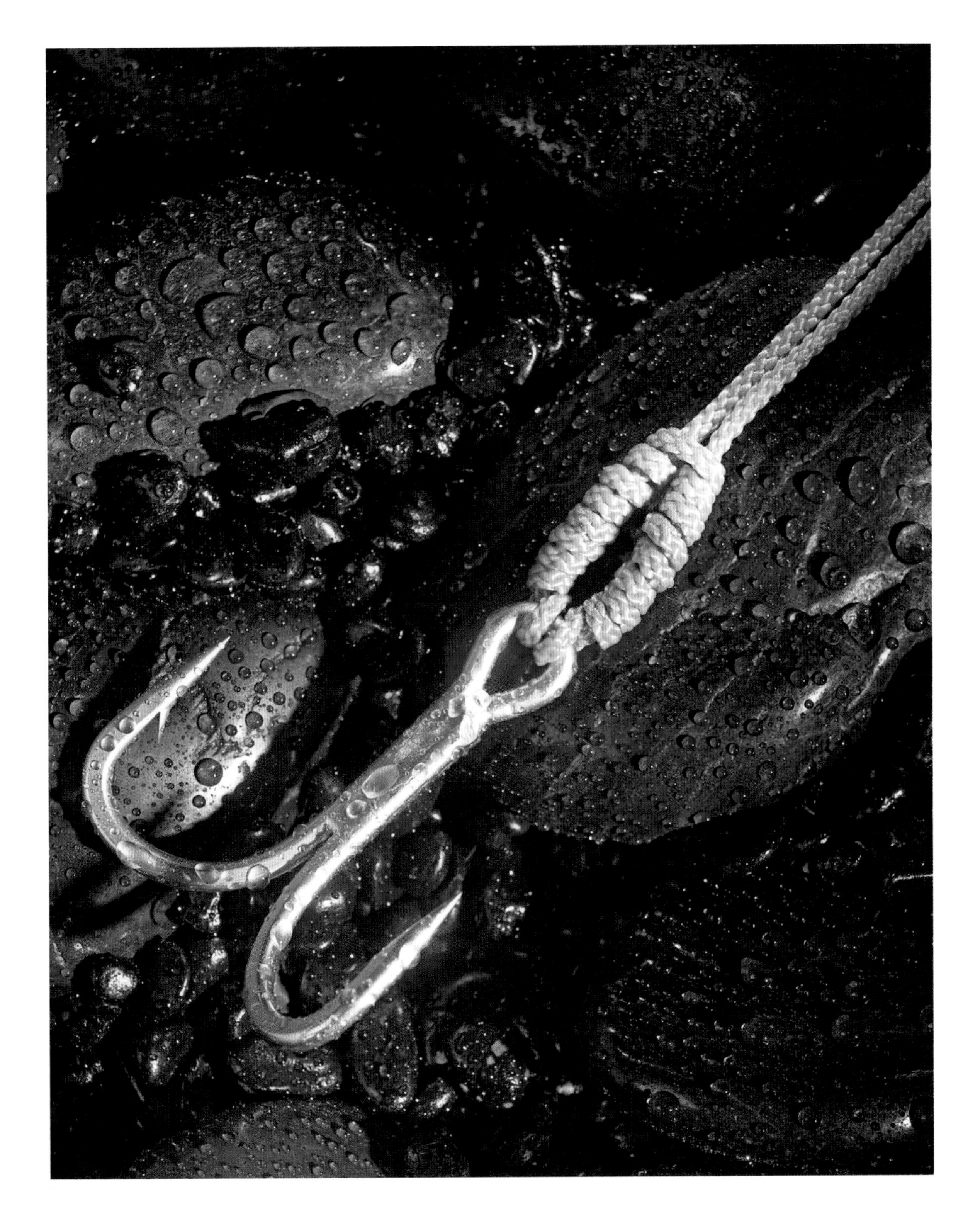

Palomar knot

This is another hook, lure, connector, or swivel knot. It is comparatively easy to tie but requires an eye or ring large enough to take a double section of line.

Knot lore
Why knots have the names they do is sometimes obscure. Mount Palomar is a peak in California, USA, and is the site of one of the world's largest reflecting telescopes.

Expert tip
This attachment consumes more of a leader line than some other knots.

1 *Make a long bight in the end of the line, tuck it through the eye or ring, and then tie an overhand knot in the doubled length.*

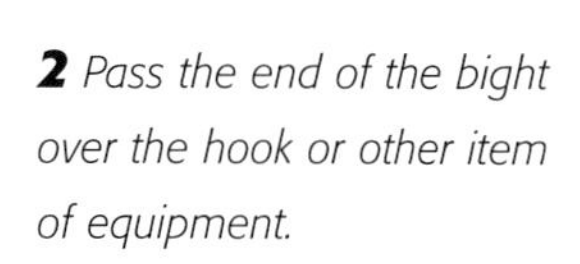

2 *Pass the end of the bight over the hook or other item of equipment.*

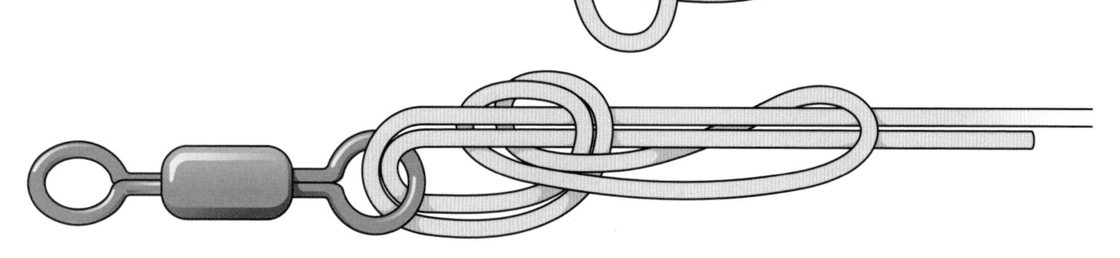

3 *Bring this loop back over the knot until it lies around the doubled standing part.*

4 *Dress and tighten the knot.*

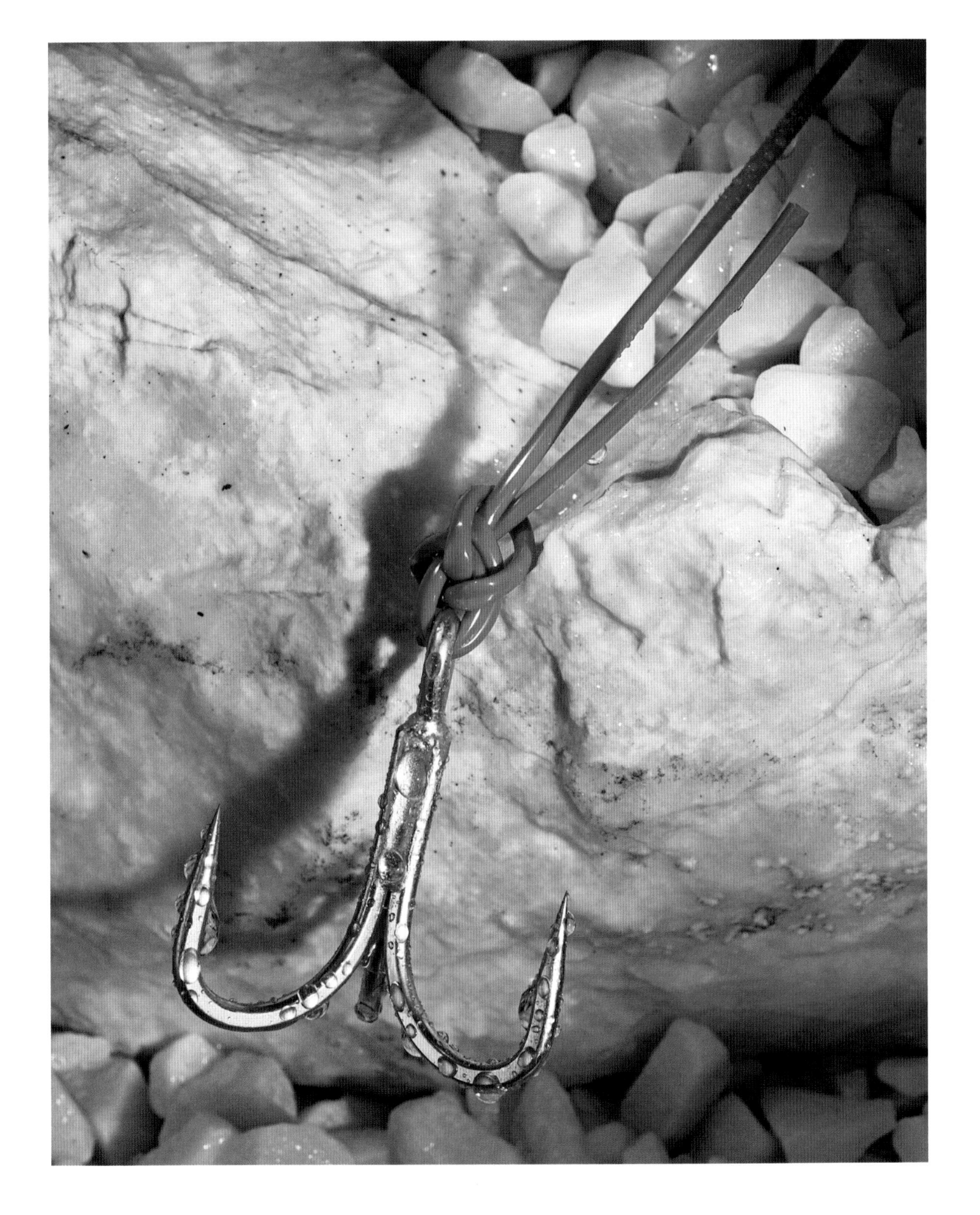

Trilene knot

Akin to the clinch knot family (already featured), this knot uses a double thickness through the eye of the hook or swivel while its tag end is tucked through the round turn.

Method #1 (basic)

1 *Take a round turn with the tag end through the eye or ring of hook or swivel, etc., then wrap and trap the standing part of the line before bringing the end back and tucking it through the round turn.*

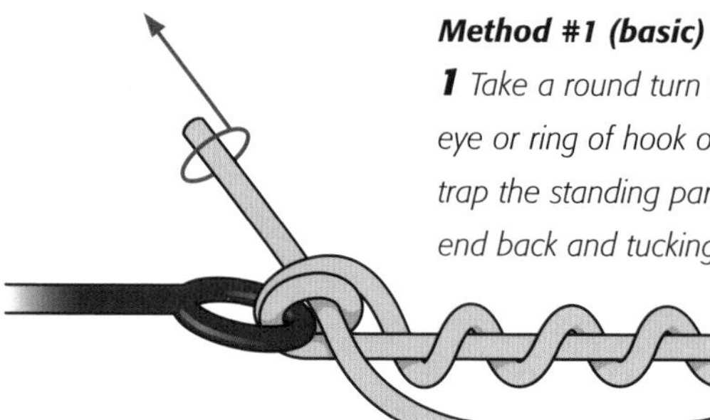

2 *Flype and tighten.*

Knot lore

This knot also goes by the trade name of Berkley trilene knot.

Expert tip

In thicker fishing lines, use less tucks to avoid problems in tightening the knot. In thinner ones, use more to retain the knot's strength and security.

Method #2 (improved)

1 *For extra security, having completed the basic knot, take the tag end and tuck it down through its own loop.*

2 *Flype and tighten the resulting knot.*

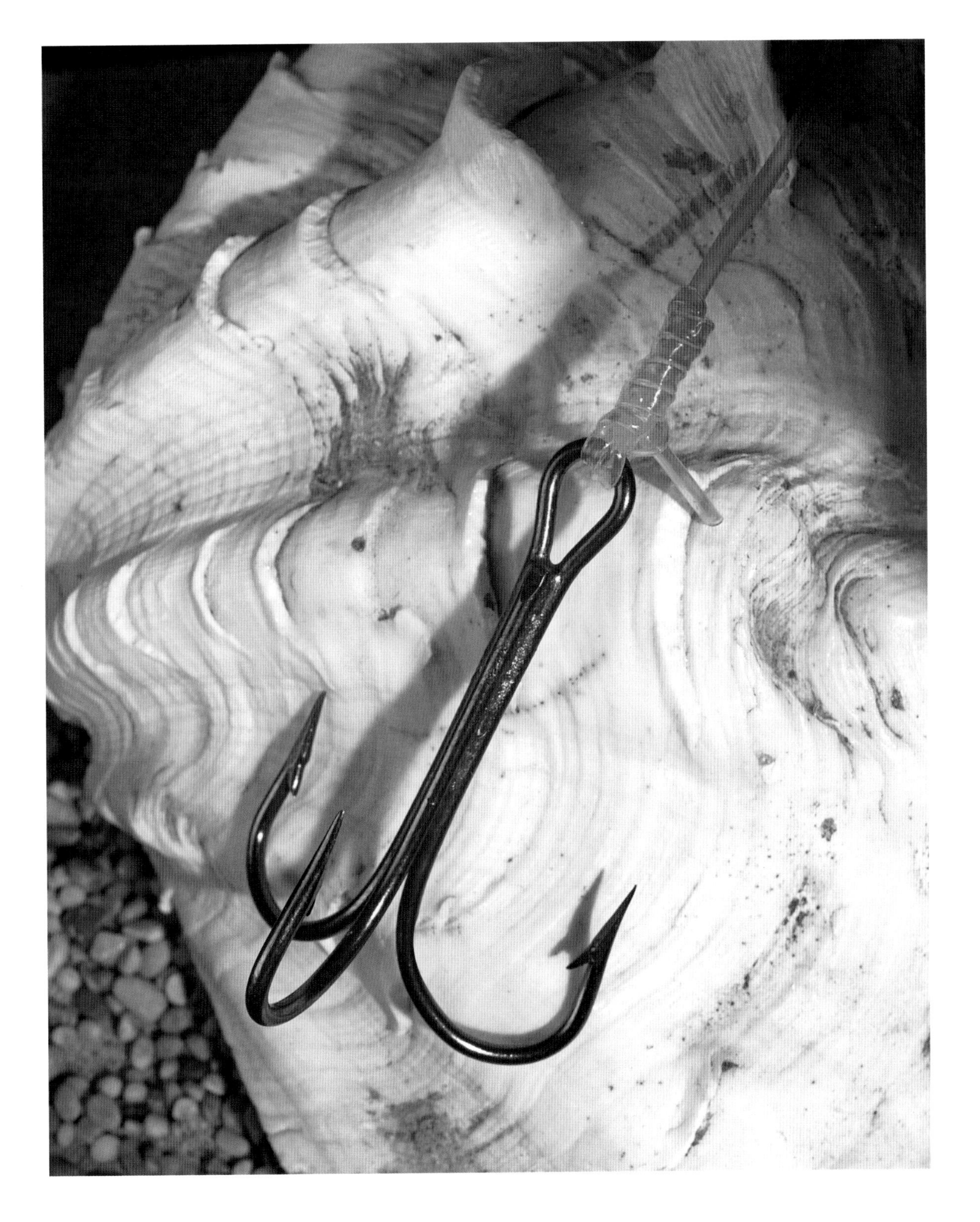

Blood knot

This is an age-old method of joining two fishing lines of similar strength, thickness, and type.

Expert tip

It is usual to ensure that the two tag ends leave the knot on opposite sides, but, if tied so that both ends emerge on the *same* side of this knot, they can be knotted together to create the 'blood loop dropper knot' (described on page 102).

Method #1 (direct)

1 *Overlap the two tag ends so that they are parallel and facing in opposite directions.*

2 *Make a series of snug wrapping turns with one end to enclose the adjacent standing part of the other line, finally tucking and trapping the end between both lines.*

3 *Repeat the process with the other tag end and tighten the knot.*

Method #2 (indirect)

1 *Overlap the two tag ends so that they are parallel and facing in opposite directions, then twist one tag end around the adjacent standing part of the other line, then bring it back and tuck it between both lines.*

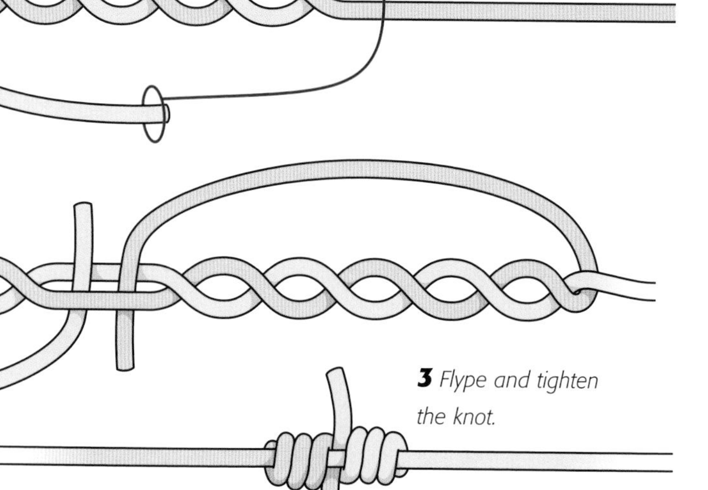

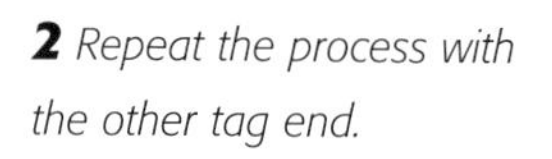

2 *Repeat the process with the other tag end.*

3 *Flype and tighten the knot.*

Surgeon's knot

This slim and streamlined knot is a strong join for fishing lines of similar type and size, and will pass readily enough through rod guides.

Knot lore

The collective term sometimes given to core-and-wrap knots like this one (and also the surgeon's loop) is 'blood knots,' but this particular knot may also be the one referred to in ancient angling texts as 'the water knot.'

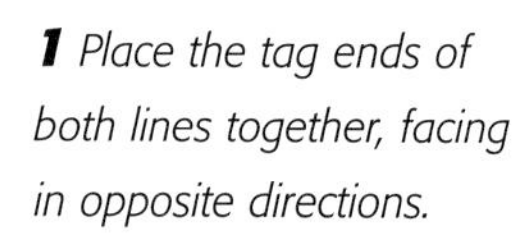

1 *Place the tag ends of both lines together, facing in opposite directions.*

2 *Tie a triple overhand knot in the doubled thickness.*

3 *Pull so as to flype the knot, letting it wrap and trap itself.*

4 *Dress and tighten carefully so that the numerous paired turns bed down snugly alongside one another.*

Expert tip

Remember that a neat and elegant knot will be stronger and more secure than one with ugly lumps resulting from careless tightening.

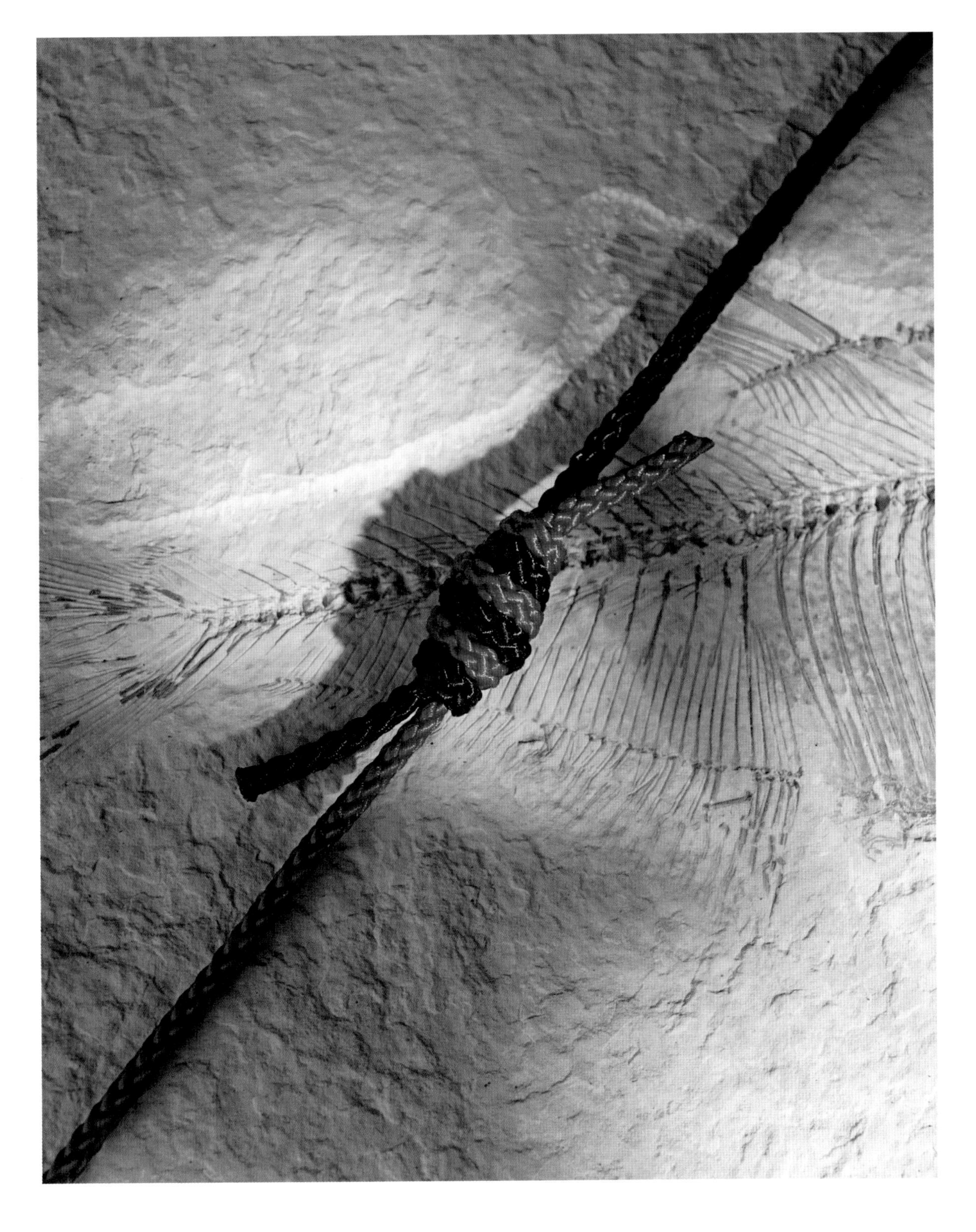

Knot locator

* May be tied in cordage or webbing
° Fishing knots

Bends (for joining together separate ends which may have to be untied later)

- Blood knot°
- Carrick bend*
- Figure-eight bend (reinforced)
- Reef knot (reinforced)
- Reever bend
- Surgeon's knot°
- Tape knot*
- Zeppelin bend

Hitches (to attach an end to a ring, rail, post, or another piece of cordage)

- Anchor (or fisherman's) bend
- Boom hitch*
- Domhof knot°
- Figure-eight becket hitch
- Fisherman's bend
- Hoisting hitch
- Hook or swivel braid knot°
- Improved basic snell°
- Improved clinch knot°
- Nail knot°
- Non-slip mono knot°
- Offshore swivel knot°
- Ossel hitch*
- Ossel knot
- Palomar knot°
- Pile hitch*
- Round turn and two half-hitches
- Trilene knot°

Fixed Loops (single, double, triple)

- Alpine butterfly loop
- Blood loop dropper°
- Bowline
- Double figure-eight loops
- Figure-eight loop*
- Frost knot*
- Overhand loop*
- Perfection loop°
- Sister loops
- Surgeon's loop°
- Triple bowline

Sliding or Adjustable Loops (or nooses)

- Scaffold knot
- Tarbuck knot

Bindings (to seize something with a short length of twine or cord)

- Common whipping
- Constrictor knot
- Double constrictor knot

Shortenings

- Braid knot
- Overhand shortening*
- Sheepshank

Stoppers

- Ashley's stopper knot
- Figure-eight stopper knot

Specialty Knots

- Alpine coil
- Asher's bottle sling
- Chinese cross knot*
- Ground line hitch (coil)*
- Knife lanyard knot
- Munter friction hitch
- Munter mule
- Turk's head (three-lead x five-bight)

Glossary of terms

Abseil (climbing) Controlled descent of a **rope**.
Anchorage (climbing) Fixed and immovable point to which to **belay**.
Belay (climbing verb) To secure a person or object with **rope**.
Bend A **knot** that binds (or bends) two separate ropes' ends together so that they may be untied again.
Bight Any slack section of a **rope** or **cord**, especially when it forms a U-shaped tongue or open **loop**.
Binding A **knot** tied in both ends of the same short length of **stuff** so as to seize anything held by it.
Blood knot Any one of several core-and-wrap knots with a characteristic appearance created by a series of wrapping turns.
Braid-on-braid The collective term for **cordage** made from a core of yarns or filaments contained within a braided outer covering or sheath.
Cable Any large **rope**, but specifically **S-laid** ropes of nine strands constructed from three **Z-laid** ropes of three strands each.
Cable-laid Construction of a **cable**.
Carabiner *See* **karabiner**.
Cord **Cordage** of less than 0.04in (10mm) diameter, smaller than a **rope**.
Cordage Term for all kinds of **rope**, **cord**, and **twine**.
Dress To manipulate a **knot** into its final form before tightening it.
Fiber The smallest component in the construction of **cordage** made from naturally occurring materials of animal or vegetable origin.
Four P's The most usual kinds of synthetic **cordage**, namely polyamide (nylon), polyester (terylene, dacron), polyethylene (polythene) and polypropylene.
Flyping Transforming a **blood knot** into its final core-and-wrap form by effectively turning it inside-out.
Hard-laid Any **cordage** rendered stiff and less flexible by tension imparted during manufacture.
Hawser-laid An almost outmoded nautical term for any **rope** of three strands, commonly **Z-laid** (or **right-handed**).
Heat sealing The process of cutting and fusing the ends of synthetic **cordage** by the application of heat.
Hitch The term for any **knot** that attaches a **rope** or **cord** to a fixed ring (or eye), rail, post, spar, or to another rope (or loop).
Hollow braid Plaited **cordage** that lacks a core.
Karabiner A snap-link of aluminum or steel, commonly oval, D-shaped, or pear-shaped, with a lockable gate.
Knot The term for any **cordage** entanglement – accidental or deliberate – that is not a **bend** or **hitch** (but including these two categories when they are tied in very small **stuff**, such as fishing **line**).
Left-handed *See* **S-laid**.
Line Any **rope** with a specific use (for example, guy-line, tow-line, laundry-line).
Loop A **bight** with a crossing point.
Monofilament A continuous extruded artificial **fiber**, the smallest element of synthetic **cordage**, circular and uniform in cross-section, with a diameter greater than 0.002 inch (50 microns).

Multifilament A cluster of extruded artificial fibers, circular and uniform in cross-section, with a diameter less than 0.002 inch (50 microns).
Natural fiber **Cordage** material of animal or vegetable origin.
Octoplait The trade name for a synthetic **cable** consisting of eight braided strands.
Rappel *See* **abseil**
Right-handed See **Z-laid**.
Rope **Cordage** over 0.4 inch (10mm) in diameter.
Sheath-and-core **Cordage**, commonly synthetic, that consists of a braided outer covering enclosing several longitudinal heart-strands.
Shroud-laid An archaic nautical term for four-strand **rope**.
S-laid **Rope** with strands that spiral counter-clockwise or **left-handed**.
Soft-laid The flexible quality of a **rope** that has been manufactured with less than average tension.
Split film The term for synthetic cordage made by first shredding and combing a sheet of polypropylene before twisting the result into yarns and strands.
Standing end The inert end of a **rope** or **cord**.
Standing part The section of any **rope** or **cord** located between the **working end** and the **standing end**.
Staplespun The construction of synthetic cordage made with monofilaments or multifilaments chopped into shorter lengths.
Strand The largest element of a **rope**, made from contra-twisted yarns.

String Domestic-quality small **stuff**, coarser than thread but sometimes equivalent to twine.
Stuff A common term for any kind of **cordage**.
Super fibers A term for types of high-performance synthetic cordage such as Kevlar, Spectra (or Dyneema), and Vectran.
Synthetics **Cordage** made from artificial fibers.
Tag end A term used in angling to mean the **working end** of a fishing **line**.
Thread Very thin **stuff** of fine quality.
Twine Very thin **stuff**, somewhat coarser than **thread**.
Whipping A **twine** or **thread binding** to keep a cut rope's end from unravelling.
Working end The end of a **rope** or **cord** that is employed in tying knots.
Yarn The basic element of any **strand** in a **rope**, spun from **natural fiber** or **synthetics**.
Z-laid **Rope** with strands that spiral clockwise (or right-handed).

Recommended reading

Ashley, Clifford W., *The Ashley Book of Knots,* published (NY, 1944) by Doubleday, Doran & Co. Inc., and (London, 1947) by Faber & Faber Ltd., with a revised 1993 edition.

Hopkins, Richard, *Knots*, published (GB, 2003) by Salamander Books Ltd. ISBN 1-84065-508-9.

Pawson, Des, *Knots & Splices*, published (GB, 2001) by PRC Publishing Ltd. ISBN 1-85648-604-4.

Perry, Gordon, *Knots*, published (GB, 2002) by Grange Books, ISBN 1-84013-493-3.

Warner, Charles, *A Fresh Approach to Knotting and Ropework*, published (NSW, Australia, 1992), ISBN 0-9592036-3-X.

Further information

The International Guild of Knot Tyers (IGKT)

One individual human lifetime is barely enough to comprehend all that there is to discover about the art, craft, and science of knotting; but devotees within the IGKT collectively strive to do so, preserving the traditional repertoire as well as devising fresh knots and innovative knotting techniques.

The Guild was established in 1982 and it is now a UK-registered educational charity with a worldwide membership. Members enjoy the quarterly magazine *Knotting Matters* which contains informed articles, expert tips, letters, editorial comment, as well as news and views on everything to do with knotting.

I know of three groups that meet regularly in the United States:

• The Texas Branch was formed as a chapter of the IGKT in February 1996. Membership has grown steadily and now also includes members from England and Tasmania. Membership of the Texas Branch is open to beginning knot tyers and experts alike.

• The Pacific Americas Branch, a chapter of the IGKT, was formed in Southern California, in January 1997 to bring a local focus for knotters in the Western US, Canada, and Alaska. It is affiliated with the Los Angeles Maritime Museum in San Pedro, California and members keep in touch with a Branch newsletter called *Knot News*.

• A local group of the IGKT-North American Branch has been formed in the Washington DC metropolitan area. The 'Mid-Atlantic Region of the NAB' meets regularly in Maryland (just outside Washington, DC), and invites IGKT members or other knotting enthusiasts to join their meetings and events.

Guild websites include:
IGKT: http://www.igkt.net
IGKT North American branch:
http://www.igktnab.org/
IGKT Pacific American branch:
http://www.igktpab.org/
IGKT Texas branch:
http://texasknot.tripod.com/

There are numerous other linked websites – a few of them animated – concerned with knotting and rope making, and those who are familiar with surfing the web can simply key 'knots' or 'rope' into a search engine and see where their searches take them. A fruitful starting point, however, would be the comprehensive treatment under three headings – knot tying, knot theory, and knot art – presented by IGKT member Peter Suber at
http://www.earlham.edu/~peters/knotlink.htm

Acknowledgements

The cordage used to illustrate the knots in this book was generously donated from three sources:

English Braids, Spring Lane, Malvern, Worcestershire, WR14 1AL, England. Tel: +44 (0)1684 892222 Fax: 01684 892111 E-mail: info@englishbraids.com Website: www.englishbraids.com

Footrope Knots, (Des and Liz Pawson) 501 Wherstead Road, Ipswich, Suffolk, IP2 8LL, England. Tel: +44 (0)1473 690 090 Email: knots@footrope.fsnet.co.uk

Jimmy Green Marine, The Meadows, Beer, East Devon Heritage Coast, EX12 3ES, England. Tel: +44 (0)1297 20744 Fax: 01297 20744 E-mail: mailorder@jimmygreen.co.uk Website: www.jimmygreen.co.uk

Index